LEARN TO TURN

Barry Gross

Fox
Chapel Publishing

1970 Broad Street • East Petersburg, PA 17520
www.FoxChapelPublishing.com

Alan Giagnocavo
Publisher

Peg Couch
Acquisition Editor

Gretchen Bacon
Editor

Troy Thorne
Design and Layout

Barry Gross/Greg Heisey
Photography

ISBN-13: 978–1–56523–273–0
ISBN-10: 1–56523–273–9

Publisher's Cataloging-in-Publication Data

Gross, Barry.
    Learn to turn / Barry Gross. -- East Petersburg, PA : Fox Chapel
Publishing, cc2005.

        p. ; cm.

        ISBN-13: 978-1-56523-273-0
        ISBN-10: 1-56523-273-9
        Includes glossary and index.

        1. Turning--Technique. 2. Woodwork. 3. Woodwork--Patterns.
4. Lathes. I. Title.

TT201 .G76 2005
684/.083--dc22   0509

To learn more about the other great books from
Fox Chapel Publishing, or to find a retailer near you,
call toll-free 1-800-457-9112 or visit us at **www.FoxChapelPublishing.com**.

Note to Authors: We are always looking for talented
authors to write new books in our area of woodworking, design,
and related crafts. Please send a brief letter describing your idea to
Peg Couch, Acquisition Editor, 1970 Broad Street, East Petersburg, PA 17520.

Printed in the United States of America
10 9 8 7 6 5 4 3 2 1

Dedication

Writing a book on woodturning takes a long time away from your family, and I am blessed with a wife and family who understand the time constraints needed to fulfill that obligation. Thank you Lenora (my best friend), who assists, guides, and offers a unique perspective to this obsession I have with turning!

Acknowledgments

First, I want to thank Alan Giagnocavo, Peg Couch, Gretchen Bacon, and the rest of the Fox Family for giving me the opportunity to produce another book on turning for Fox Chapel Publishing.

For the finer points of turning, my friend Ed Ryan has been magnanimously offering his advice and guidance to me for years. I give full credit to Ed for showing me as well as hundreds of other turners the "ABC's" of tool control. Whenever instructing students, using the "Ed Ryan" method always makes the subject of tool control much easier for students to comprehend.

The following companies and individuals, listed alphabetically, have either provided tools, supplies, or invaluable advice, and I want to thank them for their time and patience in assisting me with my questions.

Arizona Silhouette—Bill Baumbeck
Berea HardWoods—Jim Heusinger
BG Artforms
Craft Supply USA—Rex Burnham
Iron Clad Performance Wear—Kyle Jochai
New Edge Cutting Tools—Fred Smith
Oneway Manufacturing—Stephen Feringa
Packard Woodworks—Brad Packard
Penn State Industries—Ed Levy, Mark Schwartz, and Bill Whitaker
Robert Sorby Turning Tools—Peter Gill
RPM Wood Finishes Group (Behlen's Finishing Products)—Greg Williams
Trend Airshield and Trend Air Ace—Terry Cole
Triton Powered Respirator—Mark Owen
Wagner Electronic Products—Denise Padgett
WMH Tool Group (Jet Tools)—John Otto
Woodcraft Corporation—Don Guillard

About the Author

Barry Gross's love of woodworking started as a child, when he would build "boats" out of 2x4s and nails and try to float them in the bay (unsuccessfully). He purchased his first lathe at age 15 and started to turn small spindles with little success because there was no instruction available. Later on, however, Barry returned to the lathe and created many pieces of furniture for 30 years.

After taking a course on pen turning, Barry's love for turning was solidified. He has turned thousands of pens and small turnings with all types of materials. Barry also belongs to a number of local turning clubs and the American Association of Woodturners. He demonstrates turning at the *Wood Works* shows in different parts of the country and has published over 60 articles in various woodworking magazines, including *Woodturning Design*. In 2005, Barry was elected into the Who's Who in Executives and Professionals.

Table of Contents

Introduction

So much has been written about woodturning in the past that it creates a challenge to approach the topic with an innovative agenda. My method is to look at woodturning from the perspective of the student and not the teacher. Looking at woodturning from this viewpoint brings to light some of the frustrating aspects of the hobby as a beginner—such as feeling nervous when you first try to turn a piece of wood on a lathe; struggling to grind an edge on a tool; attempting to get a good finish on a bowl; or turning the final bead on a spindle, getting a "catch," and demolishing your project. I can identify with these and other apprehensions because I did them. Any experienced turner will tell you that we all make mistakes and that practice working at a particular skill is all it takes for the mistakes to correct themselves. However, by identifying some common problems and offering tips to overcome these issues, the hobby will become more enjoyable and some of the trepidation will be relieved.

So, what are you going to learn from this book? Many topics will be covered, and safety is an important issue that will be discussed. Controlling dust in your shop is especially important to your safety—it's a necessity and not a luxury! For those who have not selected a lathe, you can see what features are important to you and choose the correct lathe for your individual needs. You'll also discover what other power tools are necessary for your shop and which ones are "nice to have."

You'll learn where and how to obtain wood—from the raw log or by purchasing a prepared blank—how to select turning tools, and how to use the ABC's of tool control. Certain projects will be made with specific turning tools to enrich your tool control.

Once your project is turned, you will have to sand and finish it. Here we will discuss many different types of finishes. Once you have completed your work, how do you market the finished product? A gallery of finished work by a coalition of distinguished turners is available for admiration and for inspiration.

Finally, to me, the most important subject is troubleshooting and how to fix some of the problems you will encounter.

That's it—a big task, but one I am sure you will enjoy. Now, with all that said, we have a lot of work ahead of us, so let's have some fun and "make some dust!"

—Barry Gross

Getting Started

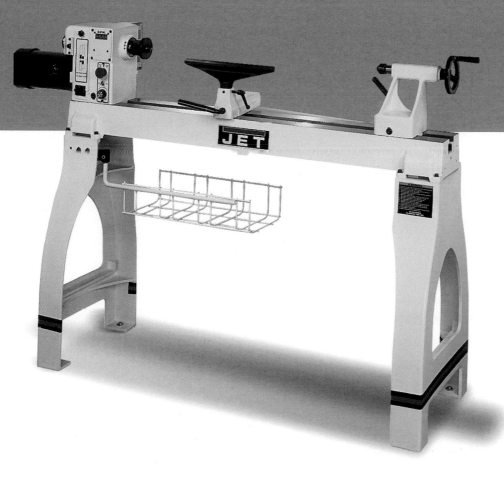

- **Safety**
- **Basic Workshop and Tools**
- **Choosing Wood**
- **Sharpening Tools**
- **Sanding**
- **Finishing**

Before you start any actual turning, you'll need to assess your tools and workshop space. For many beginners, this will mean buying tools, determining where your work space will be, and setting up your shop. As you think about what tools and space will be necessary, be certain to take safety requirements into consideration. It does not make any difference if you become the best turner the world has ever seen if you do not work safely!

Safety

A top priority for everyone who wishes to work with a lathe and the accessories that accompany this rewarding pastime must be safety. Every book on turning has a section on safety, and there is a reason for this section. Despite continued warnings, people continue to work in unsafe ways!

One important but overlooked component to safety in a workshop is the ability to turn off a piece of equipment quickly in case of an emergency. Knowing where the off switch is located for each piece of equipment or having a master kill switch installed for the entire shop can be invaluable in case of a catastrophic event. Some other general guidelines to safety are listed in the following section. While many of these items may seem like common sense, accidents still do happen.

Photo 1.1. Goggles offer better protection than regular glasses.

Eye protection

The first and foremost safety issue concerns our eyes, and as such, eye protection is a must. It can happen in an instant: A small chip of wood flies off the lathe and scratches your cornea. Then, in the back of your mind, you can hear your mother's voice telling you, "See, I told you you would poke your eye out with that thing." The moral is wear eye protection!

The first line of defense, or the very least amount of protection to wear, is safety goggles. Goggles that wrap around your face offer better protection from flying chips than regular glasses (see **Photo 1.1**). The next step up is a full face shield. Finally, the best protection is a combination full face shield, which combines sound protection and a helmet with air filtration. **Photo 1.2** shows a powered respirator. This type of respirator offers a continuous stream of filtered air flowing down inside the visor and supplying clean air for your lungs. In addition, there is built-in ear protection with the attached earmuffs.

Photo 1.2. You'll get eye, sound, and dust protection with a powered respirator.

Dust control

Controlling fine wood dust from sanding is a pressing issue that must not be ignored. Repeated exposure to dust can cause problems for the eyes, sinuses, and lungs. Watering, redness, and conjunctivitis (pink eye) are some of the possible side effects when fine sanding dust gets in your eyes. Runny noses, sneezing, breathing difficulties, and asthma attacks are other side effects that can be triggered by fine particle dust.

It's also important to note that a number of people are very allergic to certain types of dust from various exotic woods, such as cocobolo and kingwood. If you are allergic to certain types of woods, you may want to avoid them altogether. In addition, turning spalted woods can be hazardous because the fungal matter that is embedded in the wood is released when you either cut the wood with your tools or sand it with sandpaper. When this fungal dust is released into the air, it can cause serious respiratory problems.

To avoid some of these dust problems, at the very least, a washable dust mask (see **Photo 1.3**) should be worn. You could also choose a mask with replaceable filters (see **Photo 1.4**). To increase the protection level, a lightweight face shield with a built-in battery-powered air filter is a good way to combat dust and provide excellent eye protection (see **Photo 1.5**).

The next level in dust collection is to remove fine dust particles from the air as they are formed. A dust collection system, such as a shop vacuum or a larger one-horsepower, cartridge dust collector (see **Photos 1.6** and **1.7**), should be utilized. The larger dust collector in Photo 1.7 incorporates a .5 micron cartridge filter which is said to remove 99.8% of dust that is produced. In the event that the dust escapes either of these two collection systems, a ceiling-mounted dust collection unit can filter out airborne dust particles that the shop vacuum or the cartridge dust collector does not capture (see **Photo 1.8**).

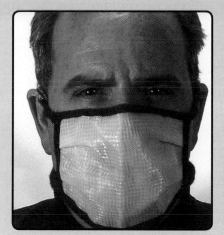

Photo 1.3. Basic dust protection with a washable dust mask.

Photo 1.4. This mask features replaceable filters.

Photo 1.5. This respirator combines a face shield with a lightweight respirator built into the head piece.

Photo 1.6. A shop vacuum can be used for smaller dust control issues.

Photo 1.8. A ceiling-mounted dust collection system can catch airborne particles that a shop vacuum or a cartridge dust collector misses.

Photo 1.7. A one-horsepower dust collection system with a cartridge filter.

Fatigue

Fatigue can be an important safety factor. If you are tired, do not attempt to start a project. If you feel tired after working in the shop for a while, stop working in the shop and get some rest; your project will still be there tomorrow. It only takes a momentary lapse of judgment for an accident to occur.

Photo 1.10. A full-length turning smock reduces the risk of loose clothing being entangled in the lathe.

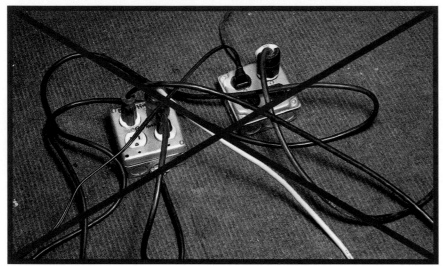

Photo 1.9. Avoid situations in which power cords can be a tripping hazard or can cause an overloaded circuit.

Electrical safety

Since every shop is not like the New Yankee Workshop, and space is often at a premium, it is important to avoid having extension cords running all over your work area, causing either a tripping hazard or a potential overloaded circuit (see **Photo 1.9**). Try to keep cords out of the way or tape them down if they must run through high-traffic areas.

Hair and clothing

Loose clothing around the lathe should be avoided, and never lean over a lathe that is running. Wearing a turning smock helps to protect against flying chips, and some smocks will even keep fine dust particles out while allowing the garment to breathe (see **Photo 1.10**).

Place long hair under a hat or tie it back, as illustrated (see **Photo 1.11**). Never allow your hair to dangle near a running lathe (see **Photo 1.12**).

Photo 1.11. Long hair should be tied back or placed under a hat.

Photo 1.12. Never let long hair near a spinning lathe!

Checking the lathe

Before turning on the lathe, double check all of the following.

■ Make sure the lathe is secured to the tabletop if it is a bench model or is securely bolted to the floor if it is a floor model.

■ Turn the hand brake to guarantee that your work does not come in contact with the tool rest or any other part of the lathe (see **Photo 1.13**). Also, make sure that you adjust the tool rest to approximately the center of the workpiece, so the work will spin evenly when the lathe is turned on (see **Photo 1.14**).

■ Ensure that the lathe speed is correctly set for the particular item you are turning. As a general rule of thumb, it's always a good idea to start at the slowest setting and increase the speed as you feel more comfortable. If your piece is not even close to being round, or "out of round," make sure that the speed is set for the slowest setting. High speeds can cause too much vibration, which is bad for the headstock and which will cause the lathe to "walk" across the floor or tabletop if it is not properly secured.

■ Make sure your tools are sharp; dull tools make it much harder to obtain a smooth cut.

■ Check your stance. You want to be comfortable when you are standing before your work. An improper stance can cause neck and back strain and lead to unnecessary fatigue. Your feet should be approximately shoulder-width apart as you stand parallel to the lathe. One hand should be resting on the tool rest, and the other hand should be holding the end of the tool near your hip. The idea is to move your body back and forth while keeping your hand close to your hip (see **Photo 1.15**).

■ Make sure that the lathe is the proper height: The center of the work should be slightly above your elbow when you are standing in front of the lathe in a relaxed position.

Photo 1.13. Notice that the wood is hitting the tool rest. *Do not allow this to happen!* Your workpiece will be mangled and the spindle could be set loose in your workshop.

Photo 1.14. Tool rest height should be set so that the tool will be at the center of the workpiece, and the tool rest should be approximately ⅛" away from the spinning work.

Photo 1.15. Make sure that you are standing in front of the lathe with your legs comfortably positioned and the handle of the lathe tool close to your hip.

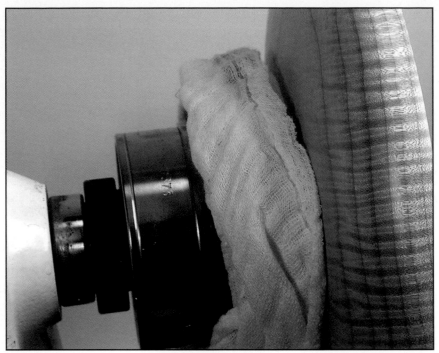

Photo 1.16. A finishing rag that "got away" from me and wrapped around the workpiece.

Photo 1.17. Wear protective boots and gloves whenever you are using a chainsaw to prepare wood for turning.

Photo 1.18. Never use a chainsaw in bare feet or with no protective gloves!

Finishing safety

When finishing a project, do not wrap any type of finishing cloth around your hand and then apply it to your work; it will inevitably get caught in your work and ruin your day (see **Photo 1.16**).

Spontaneous combustion is a very real situation that should be a concern for everyone. Follow the manufacturer's suggestions on proper disposal of finishing rags and solvents to avoid any possibility of spontaneous combustion.

Hand and foot protection

A chainsaw, either gas or electric powered, is a great tool for reducing logs or other larger pieces of wood to sizes more suitable for turning. Whenever you are using a chainsaw, protective clothing should be worn (see **Photo 1.17**). See your particular chainsaw owner's manual for the manufacturer's safety guide. As ridiculous as it sounds, never use a chainsaw in bare feet or without gloves (see **Photo 1.18**)!

Turning gloves protect against wood chips striking your hands at a high rate of speed. These are not a necessity, but the first time you turn a piece of very dry hardwood and the chips sting your hands, you will wish you had a pair of gloves to protect them. Many gloves offer high-density pads on the grips to help eliminate the vibration caused by the turning tool and subsequently will reduce cramps and hand fatigue (see **Photo 1.19**).

Photo 1.19. Use turning gloves with padded grips to reduce vibration and to protect your hands from overheated, flying chips.

Basic Workshop and Tools

First, let me say that the majority of woodturners do not all have workshops like Norm Abrams from the New Yankee Workshop and every new tool that has ever been manufactured. We make due with what we have, which usually necessitates sharing a garage with our car, a shed with our lawn mower, or a basement filled with our spouse's possessions. All of this space is room in which our spouses have graciously "allowed" us to make some dust! If space is at a premium, start out with a smaller lathe and put it on a rolling stand that can be moved around to meet your turning needs.

Shop layout

What is the best usage of space for your particular area? Your shop layout will depend on many factors; first and foremost is the size of the space. How many square feet of space will you be able to procure for your hobby? What type of turning do you want to accomplish? If you choose to turn larger projects, you'll need a larger lathe and more space than you would need for a mini-lathe that turns projects smaller than ten inches in diameter.

There are a number of books dedicated to the design and layout of workshops for every type of woodworker. We will cover some of the basics of what a good workshop should have; however, see your local library or check the Internet for more detailed information.

Whatever the final design will be for your particular workspace, one factor will remain the same: Space will be at a premium even in the most gracious of settings. With that thought in mind, a solid recommendation is to mount some of the tools that you do not use every day on rolling stands that you can roll out of the way until you choose to use them (see **Photo 1.20**).

Because your lathe will be your central tool, it is necessary that all other tools revolve around it. Set your lathe in the center of the room or in an area in which you are able to move freely around

the lathe. This way, you can use your turning tools without obstruction from any other object. Make sure that you have adequate lighting for your lathe, either near a window or under lighting from another source. Also have your turning tools in a position where you can easily reach them when they are needed, as demonstrated by the Lazy Susan-type holder in **Photo 1.21**.

Position your grinder close to your lathe so you can sharpen your tools often. It is inefficient to walk from one end of your shop to the other just to put an edge on a skew to finish a cut.

Photo 1.21. A Lazy Susan can be a convenient way to retrieve your tools when needed.

Photo 1.20. At the left is an oscillating spindle sander and at the right a router/shaper. To save valuable space in the shop, mount tools on rolling stands so that they can be rolled out and used when needed and placed back under the workbench when they're not in use.

Choosing a Lathe

Obviously, the first tool that you'll need to consider purchasing is a lathe. Lathes can be broken down into two main types: free standing and bench mounted. All lathes have a few common parts, such as a headstock, a tailstock, and a tool rest (see the Parts of a Lathe diagram below). How each lathe is manufactured, where the controls are mounted, how powerful the motor is, what type of steel is used, and many other salient features are utilized by each manufacturer to distinguish one manufacturer's product from another's.

Parts of a Lathe

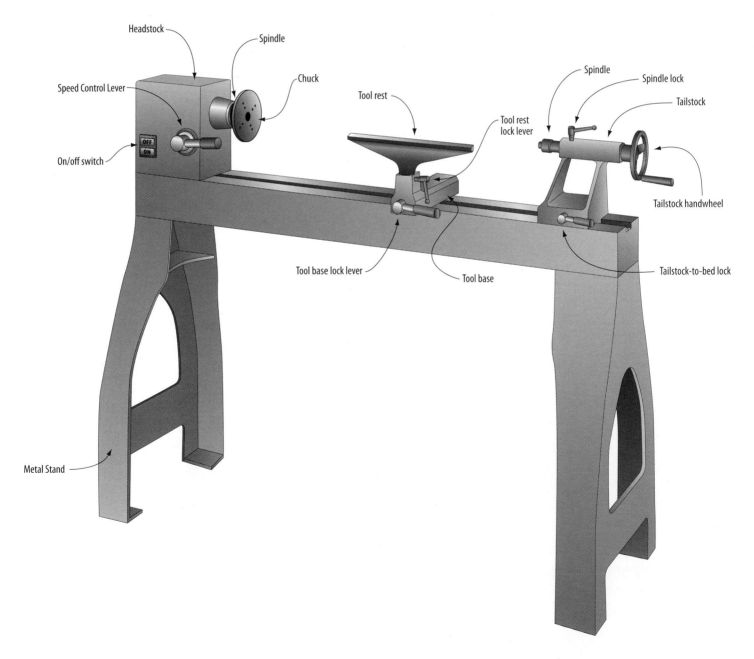

To me, choosing a lathe is the equivalent of choosing a car: You can choose from an economy, a mid-range, or a luxury model to fit your budget requirements. An axiom that holds true with any purchase is "purchase the best you can afford." Do not always go with the least expensive—especially with tools. You will regret it later!

The best way to choose a lathe is to try it before you buy it. Did you ever purchase a car without test-driving it? Any sales representative can make his product look or perform great—that is why he is selling it. However, you should not purchase a lathe unless you try it before you take it home. Stand in front of the lathe as you would when you are turning. Try the controls, making sure that you can easily reach them. Turn the unit on and off, increase the speed, move the hand wheel brake, move the tailstock—just try the lathe. If it does not feel comfortable to you, do not purchase it.

Another way to research a lathe purchase is to visit a turning club. There are turning clubs all across America and many internationally. The American Association of Woodturners is an excellent resource for information on local chapters. Go to a meeting and find out what other people own and how they like their lathes. Ask questions of the members, pick up a woodturning magazine, or go to the Internet for information. Don't just purchase the first lathe you see!

One quick trick I like to do before I purchase a lathe is check to see if the tailstock and the headstock line up properly. To perform this test,

put the drive spur into the headstock, bring the tailstock up to the headstock drive spur, and see if they both line up "point to point," as illustrated in **Photo 1.22**. If they do not line up, your work will never be symmetrical.

Finally, think about what type of turning you are interested in accomplishing. Do you want to turn large bowls, long spindles, or miniatures? How about making pens? You should answer these and other questions before you purchase the lathe. If you want to turn large objects, make sure you purchase a lathe that is heavy and well constructed. On the other hand, if you are strictly going to do miniatures, then a mini-lathe is your best choice.

To assist you with purchasing a new lathe, I've included some general information on the different lathe types on page 10. Look at the information, and then go and try the different lathes at various woodworking locations.

One final important feature is the reputation of the woodworking facility and how comfortable you feel purchasing the lathe from this individual or establishment.

Photo 1.22. Point-to-point test: Check to see if the tailstock and headstock line up before purchasing a lathe.

Types of Lathes

Individual lathes come in a variety of sizes with a wide range of features.
Here's a quick look at some of the common categories and their general characteristics.

Photo courtesy Bonnie Klein

Miniature Lathe

A true miniature lathe has a swing of 4 to 5 inches, and the length between centers is 6 to 12 inches. They are quite portable due to their small weight—usually around 30 to 40 pounds. Miniature lathes are typically used to turn genuinely miniature items, like knobs and dollhouse furniture.

Mini Lathe

These lathes have a swing around 10 inches and a length between centers around 14 inches. Horsepower usually runs around ½ hp. These lathes are good to learn on and are great for teaching children how to turn. They're also very popular with pen turners.

Bench Lathe

The lathes in this category run the gamut from small to large lathes. As these are more affordable than floor lathes, many turners choose to begin their turning careers with benchtop lathes. This type of lathe is often used to turn a wide variety of projects. It is relatively easy to build a stand for a bench lathe and then adjust it to your height. If you do build a stand, make sure it is a very sturdy one that will be able to withstand the vibration from an out-of-round object.

Floor Lathe

These come in a wide variety of sizes; floor lathes can be mini lathes with legs or huge industrial-sized production lathes. Swing can be anywhere from 10 to 24 inches, and the distance between centers can be as small as 14 inches and as large as 8 feet. Likewise, hp ranges from ½ to 3. Like benchtop lathes, these lathes are typically used to turn a wide variety of projects.

Turning tools and lathe accessories

Other than a lathe, what are some of the basic tools needed for turning in a workshop? Some of the first tools you'll want to consider are turning tools and the different types of accessories for your lathe.

Turning Tools

The first basic tools needed are a good set of turning tools. Once you decide what type of turning you wish to complete—bowls, spindles, hollow vessels, boxes, pens, or other miniatures—you can determine exactly what tools will be the best for your particular needs.

A good basic set of turning tools (see the Basic Woodturning Tools sidebar) should consist of a roughing gouge, a bowl gouge, a skew (either oval or straight), a parting tool, a spindle gouge, and a round nose scraper. One other tool that I recommend is called a Spindlemaster. This tool combines a skew (which may be tough to handle for beginners) and a spindle gouge into one convenient tool (see **Photo 1.23**).

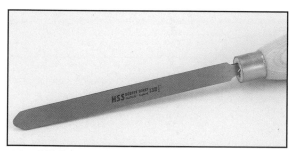

Photo 1.23. For those individuals who are "skew challenged," a Spindlemaster is a useful tool combining a spindle gouge and a skew without the fear of the dreaded catches associated with a regular skew.

There are many excellent manufacturers of turning tools on the market today. When choosing a set of turning tools, make sure that the tools are manufactured from a high grade of steel, such as M2, or from Powered Metallurgy steel. M2 high-speed steel is now the standard for turning tools and can hold an edge up to six times longer than regular carbon steel. Turning tools produced

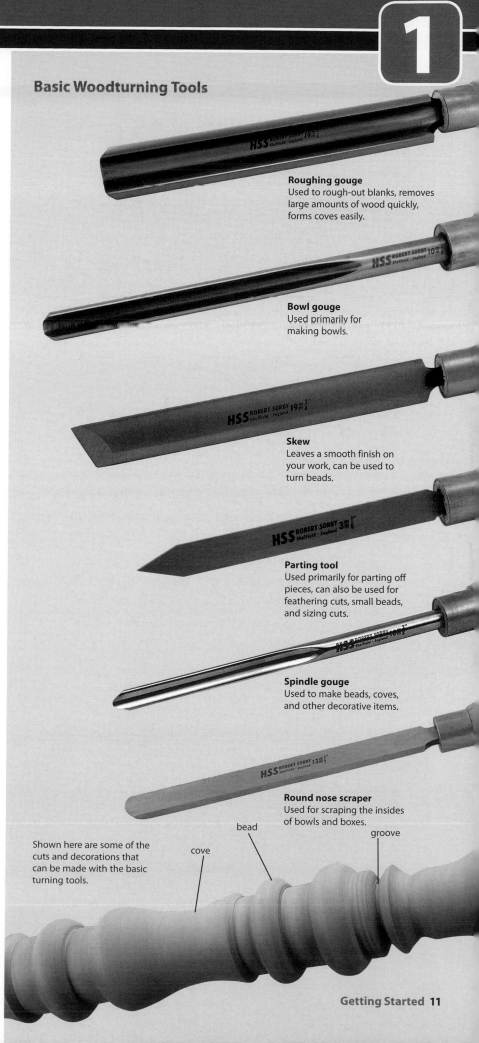

Basic Woodturning Tools

Roughing gouge
Used to rough-out blanks, removes large amounts of wood quickly, forms coves easily.

Bowl gouge
Used primarily for making bowls.

Skew
Leaves a smooth finish on your work, can be used to turn beads.

Parting tool
Used primarily for parting off pieces, can also be used for feathering cuts, small beads, and sizing cuts.

Spindle gouge
Used to make beads, coves, and other decorative items.

Round nose scraper
Used for scraping the insides of bowls and boxes.

Shown here are some of the cuts and decorations that can be made with the basic turning tools.

cove
bead
groove

Photo 1.24. Some tools offer long-lasting, disposable carbide-coated tips for those individuals who do not want to sharpen their turning tools or who have a difficult time putting a good edge on their tools. When the tip gets dull, simply throw it away and get a new tip.

from Powered Metallurgy steel are said to hold an edge three to four times longer than that of M2 steel tools. Both steels are good, but which is better for you? Do yourself a favor and try them both at the woodturning store before you purchase.

Tools with replaceable carbide tips, such as New Edge cutting tools, are a new technological advancement on the market (see **Photo 1.24**). These tools are guaranteed to always have a fresh cutting edge and are made for the person who is "sharpening challenged." When the carbide tip gets dull (which will take a long time), just throw it away, purchase a new carbide tip, and replace the old one.

Chucks, Drive Spurs, and Faceplates

There are many ways to secure your workpiece to the headstock, and the most common is with

a chuck. A chuck is a device that will hold your workpiece in place while you are turning.

Before purchasing a chuck, determine what type of turning you will do. Will you turn larger pieces, smaller pieces, bowls, pens? Large projects will require larger chucks, and smaller projects will be easier on smaller chucks. There are also specialty devices available for specific projects. Pen turning mandrels, for example, are primarily used to turn pens. Also, consider the type of lathe that you will be using. You won't want to turn a large, heavy chuck on a mini-lathe; doing so will only wear out the bearings in the headstock very quickly.

There are generally three basic types of devices for holding your workpiece: those used for spindle turning, those used for faceplate turning, and those used for specialty turning. Drive spurs (see **Photo 1.25**) are generally used for spindle turning (turning in which the workpiece is held between the headstock and the tailstock with the grain running parallel to the bed). This type of mounting device fits into the headstock spindle.

Faceplates are generally used for faceplate turning (turning in which the workpiece is usually

Photo 1.25. Pictured here is a variety of mounting devices. The Jacobs Chuck holds a drill in the headstock or the tailstock. The others pictured mount the workpiece on the lathe.

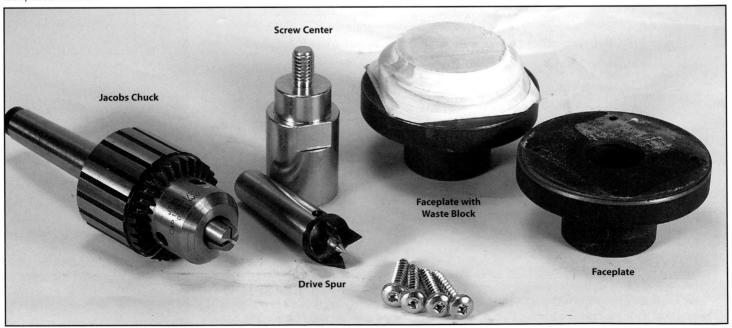

Screw Center

Jacobs Chuck

Faceplate with Waste Block

Drive Spur

Faceplate

Four-Jawed Chuck with Spigot Jaws

Jumbo Jaw

Single-Hand Key

Four-Jawed Chuck with Center Wood-Worm Screw

Photo 1.26. Assorted chucks and jaws used to hold faceplate work. The single-hand key operates all three chucks.

held by only the headstock and the grain runs perpendicular to the bed). Blocks of wood mounted on faceplates with special double-faced turning tape can serve as waste blocks (see Photo 1.25). Others use screws to mount the workpiece to the faceplate. Four-jawed chucks (see **Photo 1.26** and **Photo 1.27**) have four jaws that open and close to help hold the workpiece.

Other specialty devices include Jacobs chucks (see Photo 1.25), which hold a drill in the head-stock or the tailstock to make drilling easier and pen mandrels (see **Photo 1.28**), which are rods mounted between centers and used to turn hollow pieces. These are just some of the tools that you can use to assist you in creating turned objects that will amaze your friends and family.

There are many different manufacturers and types of chucks available on the market today that are specifically designed for your particular type of turning, so decide what type of turning you will do and purchase the correct chuck for your application. If you are unsure, ask other woodturners or visit a local woodworking shop for advice. As you turn more items and decide what types of turning you prefer, you'll discover what types of chucks are most beneficial to you.

Photo 1.27. A four-jawed chuck secures a bowl with a spigot for faceplate turning.

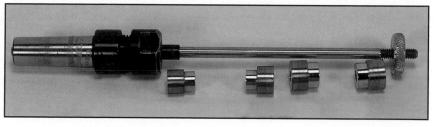

Photo 1.28. Mandrels allow you to turn hollow objects, such as pens.

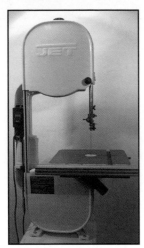

Photo 1.29. A band saw is a great tool for cutting larger pieces of wood into suitable pieces of turning stock.

Other shop tools

Other than your lathe and the turning tools used with it, you'll find that a number of other tools will make your hobby much more enjoyable. Following are just a few to consider.

Band Saw

A band saw is used to transform wood into suitable blanks for turning. There are many good-quality band saws on the market today, so, if you are purchasing one, make sure that it suits your particular turning requirements. A 12-inch band saw is a good starting point; however, if you want to turn larger bowls, you will need a larger band saw. The band saw pictured is a 14-inch band saw with a 6-inch riser block that allows for taller pieces of wood to be cut on the saw (see **Photo 1.29**). Because it is a 14-inch band saw, it can cut a piece of wood up to 28 inches in diameter—14 inches on either side of the blade—which is a huge bowl! A 12-inch band saw can cut a piece of wood 24 inches in diameter—12 inches on either side of the blade—and a 10-inch band saw can cut wood 20 inches in diameter.

Photo 1.30. Chainsaws, either electric (top) or gas (bottom), can reduce logs to smaller, more manageable pieces of wood.

Chainsaw

The million-dollar question is, "Do I use a gas-powered chainsaw or an electric-powered chainsaw (see **Photo 1.30**)?" If you will be traveling into the woods to cut your own logs, an electric one obviously will not do unless you have the world's longest extension cord! Chainsaws are great for taking logs and reducing them to workable pieces of wood that you can then cut into turnable blanks on your band saw.

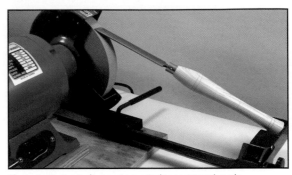

Photo 1.31. A grinding system grinds consistent bevels on your tools.

Bench Grinder

A bench grinder is necessary for sharpening your turning tools to a fine edge, unless you are using tools with replaceable carbide tips. Dull tools are dangerous and can cause problems, such as tear-out and fatigue. Many different jigs can be purchased to sharpen all of the different turning tools, but a grinding system, such as the Wolverine Grinding System (see **Photo 1.31**), is one of the most comprehensive and easiest methods to use. Sharpening your tools can be a challenging task if you let it; therefore, an entire section of this book (see the Sharpening Tools section on page 20) will be devoted to taking the fear out of sharpening your tools.

Dividers and Calipers

Dividers (see **Photo 1.32**) are used to mark bowl blanks and to scribe lines in the centers of faceplate work. Calipers (see **Photo 1.33**) are used to set diameters on spindle work.

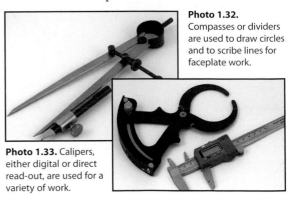

Photo 1.32. Compasses or dividers are used to draw circles and to scribe lines for faceplate work.

Photo 1.33. Calipers, either digital or direct read-out, are used for a variety of work.

Choosing Wood

Almost all civilizations and religions, from the Ancient Greeks to the Native American Indians, had beliefs that trees possessed great mysterious powers and were symbols of strength. The Celts planted trees as early as 600 BC in the names of their children to ensure a connection between the divine and the earthbound portions of the soul. It is no wonder why this fascination with trees continues today.

Numerous sources estimate that there are in excess of 50,000 species of trees currently known. Consequently, with this large a selection, where do you begin to choose what type of wood to turn? A suggestion would be to start with the most abundant source of wood that is available for you locally. In my area, local wood would include maple, cherry, or walnut. Attend a local turning meeting to find out where the members get their wood, and you will be amazed on just how much "free" wood is available for your turning pleasure. Feel free to experiment with many different types of woods, and eventually you will settle in with your "favorite" woods in which to create your own masterpieces.

Bought vs. found wood

There are generally two ways in which you can obtain wood for turning: You can buy it or you can cut it yourself. For the beginner, buying blanks may be the way to go if you're not yet ready to cut your own wood. There are many sources for ready-made bowl, vessel, and pen blanks and literally thousands of websites that sell ready-made blanks (see **Photo 1.34**). See page 110 for some resources to get you started.

Once you're comfortable, however, found wood can be a great source of blanks for your projects. In the following sections, I'll get you started with some tips and techniques to create your own blanks from logs and other found wood.

Photo 1.34. Ready-made blanks can be purchased by mail order. The tall piece is orange agate, the one to the left is Australian myrtle burl, the one to the right is Australian eucalyptus burl, and the one in the front is Bethlehem olive wood.

Transforming logs into suitable turning material

Because found wood can be a great source of turning material, especially for bowls or vessels, it's a good idea to learn how to transform a log into a turning blank. This process is often difficult for beginners to envision. Which way do I cut it? How thick should I make it? How tall do I want the piece to be? Do I want to make a bowl blank or a hollow form vessel blank? Most of your questions can be answered by really studying the log that you are about to dissect and picturing in your mind where each bowl or vessel will be within the log (see the demonstration on pages 18 and 19).

Sections of logs can be reduced into turning blanks from just about any tree (see **Photo 1.35**). Some trees may be more difficult to cut because of the hardness of the tree, such as osage orange. Even spalted trees can be made into suitable turning material; however, caution should be used when trying to make turning blanks from spalted material due to the fungal spores released when you cut the wood. Cutting spalted material for your first attempt may be difficult because the material may seem solid on the outside, but it could be so soft and "punky" on the inside of the log that it will fall apart. Avoid logs with any splits and cracks because these pieces have a tendency to fall off the lathe when you turn them.

Blanks from Burls

Burls are my personal favorite when it comes to material from which to create a blank for turning. A burl is basically a benign tree tumor (see **Photo 1.36**). It occurs when a twig bud fails to grow normally into the tissues needed to form a limb. Instead, the twig bud goes "nuts" and continually multiplies its bud cells, growing in every direction with very irregular grain structure. This irregular grain structure gives the burl its beauty.

Choose your favorite burl and follow the steps on pages 18 and 19 to reduce a log to turnable blanks (see **Photo 1.37**).

Photo 1.35. Here are three bowl blanks and one hollow vessel blank that were prepared from logs only a few short minutes before this photo was taken.

Moisture content

When you are working with found wood, it is important to determine how much moisture your wood has. For turning, you generally want blanks that are neither too wet ("green") nor too dry.

If you plan to use a lot of found wood, rather than ready-made blanks, a moisture meter is a good investment. Many meters will read the moisture content of the wood to a depth of 1½". If your blank is thicker than 1½", turn the piece over and check the bottom of the wood. This effectively gives you a reading of 3" in depth. The reading is not exact, but it can help you to decide whether a piece of wood you want to turn is dry enough or still too wet. Most manufacturers of moisture meters include a list of woods and their suggested moisture content readings in the package with their meter. Because the values for each wood and each meter vary, it is difficult to suggest any general guidelines here.

The burl blank I cut earlier (see Photo 1.37) had a moisture reading of 11.8% (see **Photo 1.38**) because it has been on my wood rack for over three years and is drying nicely. The log that was just cut (see Step 12 on page 19) has a moisture reading of 19.8% (see **Photo 1.39**). When it is turned, more moisture will be released from that blank than the maple burl blank. Additional moisture may cause a blank to warp slightly.

To prevent your prepared blank from warping, rough turn the blank down to approximately 1" thick and check the moisture content. Wrap the blank in a brown paper bag and place it in a cool, dry place. Allow it to "air dry" for approximately four to five months; then, re-check the moisture content. If the blank is sufficiently dry, continue turning it to the final thickness.

Photo 1.36. Far left is an oak burl; in the middle and to the right are two maple burls.

Photo 1.37. This prepared maple burl blank was cut from the raw burl.

Photo 1.38. The moisture meter shows a low moisture content from only the top portion of the maple burl. Each manufacturer will supply a reference chart listing each individual wood and its relative moisture content.

Photo 1.39. The moisture meter shows a higher moisture content from only the top portion of a different maple burl.

Creating Bowl Turning Blanks from a Log

1 Once you find a log to transform into turning material, check the ends for splits or large cracks that will prevent you from using any sections. If an end is cracked and checked badly, cut it back about two to three inches to avoid the cracks and to obtain a solid piece of lumber.

2 When the cracked end is cut off, look at the log and draw a line to one side of the pith (the mark to the left of the line) of the tree. If you leave the pith in your bowl blank, the chances of the bowl cracking will greatly increase.

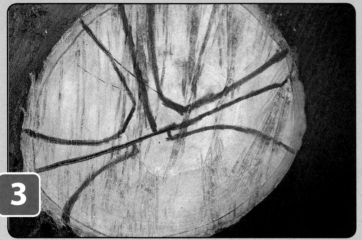

3 Using a crayon or marker, draw the general shapes of your future projects on the end of the log. Illustrated are three natural-edge bowl shapes.

4 Cut the log based on your marks. Here I am splitting the top half of my log as I marked in Step 3.

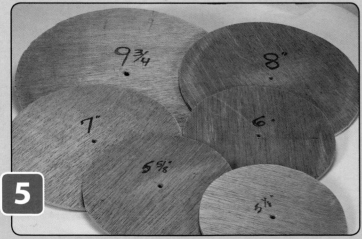

5 Prepare a number of bowl turning templates in advance made from ⅛" plywood or Plexiglas. I like to have a number of different diameters ready.

6 Place the appropriate guide on top of the cut log to ensure that you have enough clearance on each side of your template. If the template is too large, choose a smaller one that will fit your cut log.

7 If you are not going to turn this green piece of log immediately, you will have to seal the ends with wood sealer to prevent the checking and cracking of your blank. It is advisable to spread some of the sealer on the sides of the blank as well.

8 Take your cut log to your band saw and once again make sure that the template you choose will fit inside the ends of the log.

9 Turn over the blank and rest the flat portion on the table of the band saw. Then fix the appropriate template guide to your blank with a small screw. **Caution:** Do not try to cut the blank with the curved side of the log down on the table of the band saw. Always cut a log flat side down.

10 Carefully cut around the template, trying not to cut it with the band saw.

11 Here is your finished blank. Again, if you are not going to turn this piece immediately, coat the ends and one inch down the sides with wood sealer and place the blank in a cool, dry location to dry naturally.

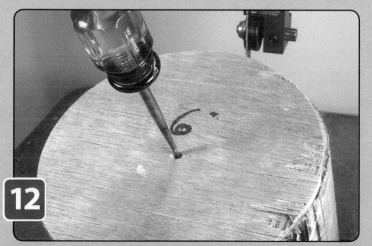

12 Once the piece is dry enough for turning, you'll need to find the center. Since you have the approximate center on the top of the blank from the screw that held the template, turn over the blank, lay the template on the bottom, and use an awl to scribe a center in the bottom of the piece.

Sharpening Tools

In sharpening, just remember one simple rule—a sharp tool is a good tool and a dull tool is an awful tool! As an instructor, one of the first questions I get asked by novice turners is, "How often should I sharpen my turning tools?" As that question is being asked and answered, I sometimes hear other students brag by saying, "I hardly ever sharpen my tools," or "I didn't know you had to sharpen them that often." As a general rule, you should sharpen your tools as soon as they get dull.

Dull tools can create a potentially dangerous situation. Obviously, a dull tool will not give you as clean a cut as a sharp tool, causing you to tear at the fibers of the wood rather than to slice them cleanly. In addition, more effort and pressure must be exerted when using a dull tool, and this may result in your becoming fatigued or ruining the project. The way the tool performs and the look of its edge will give you clues as to how sharp it is. We'll cover these aspects in more detail as we look at sharpening the individual tools.

Tools for sharpening

A good sharpening system contains a number of tools to help you sharpen your tools accurately and efficiently. Since one of the most challenging parts of turning is the ability to keep a sharp edge on your turning tools, a good grinding system is a worthwhile investment. It will help you to obtain a sharp edge on your tools, giving you every possible advantage for success.

General Sharpening Supplies

- Bench grinder and grinding wheels (80 and 120 grit)
- Grinding jig, skew, and attachment, such as the Vari-Grind attachment
- Turning tools
- Diamond wheel dresser
- Protractor, square, or angle gauge

Grinders

There are both dry grinding systems and wet grinding systems. Some turners prefer sharpening tools with a wet system because they feel that, by sharpening the tool in a reservoir of water, it offers a better edge than a dry system and avoids heat generation and loss of temper. While the wet system may have these advantages, a dry system offers convenience, speed, and reliability. Because of these factors, we will only cover the dry system here.

Photo 1.40. Choose a grinder with at least a ½ hp motor and 8" wheels. This particular model has two speeds and is attached to a plywood frame.

The first decision to make when choosing a dry grinding system is whether to have a floor-mounted grinder or a bench-mounted grinder. Your choice will largely be a matter of personal preference. Whichever one you choose, make sure that it has at least a ½ hp motor and uses 8" wheels (see **Photo 1.40**).

Grinding Wheels

Grinding wheels are an integral part of the grinding process and are offered in several different grits. However, for beginners, the basic grits of 80 (for shaping) and 120 (for finishing) will give you excellent results (see **Photo 1.41**). An important first step to successful grinding is to "balance" your grinding wheels. Balancing your wheels will make them last longer, offer a better finish on your tools, and help to eliminate vibration. Vibration can cause poor finishes on your tools, and eventually, if the vibration is serious enough, it may destroy the bearings and housings on your grinder. Balancing your grinding wheels is easily completed per the manufacturer's instructions (see **Photo 1.42**).

Wheel Dressers

Wheel dressers are used to condition and enhance the grinding performance of your grinding wheels in order to rid them of metal particles and other debris that stick to them. An accurately dressed (cleaned) wheel will grind cooler, last longer, and offer you a better finish on your tools.

A good grinding wheel should be flat—not concave—across the face of the wheel in order to perform sharpening operations quickly and efficiently without burning the edges of your tool. Currently a diamond dresser is the most effective and efficient tool for this task. One type of diamond dresser (see **Photo 1.43**) uses a single-point diamond held in an adjustable arm that is

Photo 1.41. Three 8" grinding wheels with different grits: 60 grit (gray), 80 grit (pink), and 120 grit (white).

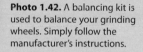

Photo 1.42. A balancing kit is used to balance your grinding wheels. Simply follow the manufacturer's instructions.

Photo 1.43. This dresser uses a single-point diamond held in an adjustable arm.

Photo 1.44. In this close-up, you can see that the diamond dressing tip is removing small amounts of the grinding wheel.

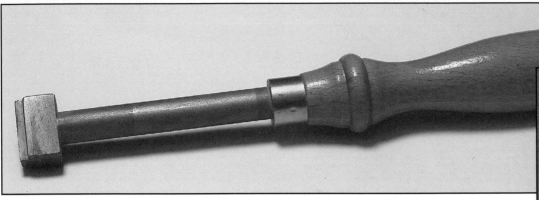

Photo 1.46. The large surface area makes this dresser quite efficient.

Photo 1.45. This dresser features a large surface that comes in contact with the wheel.

moved across the face of the wheel, producing a wheel face that is clean and flat. The jig can be adjusted in or out to take either a heavy cut or cuts as light as .003 of an inch (see **Photo 1.44**).

Another type of wheel dresser, such as the Diamond Jim, (see **Photo 1.45**) has diamond chips embedded into the surface of the dresser. This type of dresser relies on many diamond chips (this one has 1.3 karats worth!) suspended in a matrix at the top of a 1"-wide head that offers a large surface to contact the grinding wheel, making it an efficient way to grind a smooth, flat surface on your wheel (see **Photo 1.46**).

Grinding Jig

A grinding jig is a way to place your turning tools to the grinding wheel at an angle that you feel is best for your particular style of turning (see **Photo 1.47**). There are several commercial grinding systems currently available. The grinding system shown will grind gouges, scrapers, and skews, as well as other carving tools. By using a grinding system like this one, you will be able to achieve repeatable angles with minimal grinding wheel and tool wear, which is important when you first are starting with woodturning.

Photo 1.47. A grinding system like this one makes it easy to get accurate, repeatable angles on your turning tools.

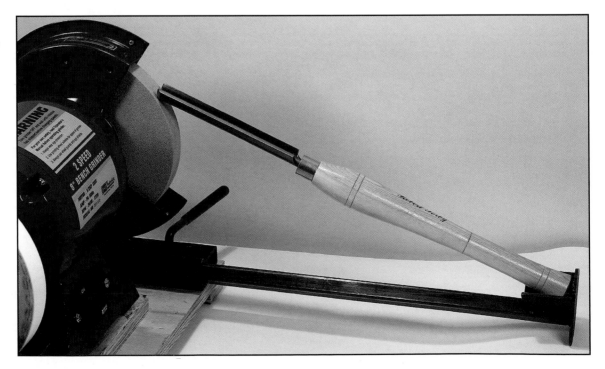

Sharpening your tools

Once you have your sharpening system set up, take a look at your tools. **Photos 1.48** and **1.49** show a bowl gouge. If your tool is sharp, you should see no light reflecting from the top of the tool (see Photo 1.48). If you see light reflecting back from the edge of the tool, then the tool needs to be sharpened further (see Photo 1.49). The easiest way for beginners to achieve repeatable results when first starting to use a grinding system is to use the same angle that was set for the tool by the manufacturer when the turning tool was purchased. Use a protractor, a square, or an angle gauge to check your tools. When you gain more experience with grinding bevels, you can change the angles to suit your particular turning needs. Now let's sharpen each of the basic turning tools.

Photo 1.48. A properly sharpened tool shows no shiny surface on the edge of the tool.

Photo 1.49. A shiny edge like this one is a tell-tale sign that this tool needs to be sharpened.

Parting Tool – 25 degrees

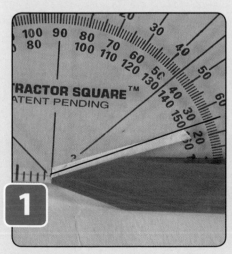

1

The typical angle for the parting tool is 25 degrees.

2

Make sure that the platform is set at a 90 degree angle to the grinding wheel.

3

Hold the parting tool flat on the platform and lightly touch the parting tool against the grinding wheel to sharpen the tool.

Roughing Gouge – 45 degrees

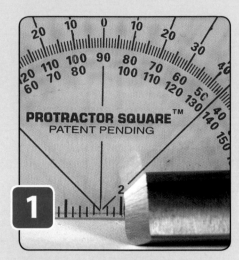

1 Use the same bevel that the manufacturer used for the roughing gouge. Typically the angle for the roughing gouge is 45 degrees.

2 Next, mark the bevel of the roughing gouge with a marker.

3 Line up the bevel with the wheel.

4 Use your hand to rotate the wheel and lightly touch the gouge to the grinding wheel to rub off the marker.

5 Examine the gouge's bevel to see where the marker was rubbed off. If the wheel rubbed off the marker on the bottom of the bevel, move the jig out slightly in order to get even contact with the entire bevel. If the top of the tool was rubbed off, move the jig in slightly to get the bevel even with the wheel. Once the correct angle has been established, continue grinding the entire length of the bevel with a side-to-side motion.

6 The corners tend to grind slower than the middle of the tool, so grind the edges slightly longer to maintain a square edge across the top of the gouge.

Spindle Gouge–35 degrees, Bowl Gouge–50 to 55 degrees

Though they are typically ground to different angles, the spindle gouge and the bowl gouge are sharpened in much the same way. Use a marker to mark the bevel of the spindle gouge and place the gouge into the pocket of the jig. Rub the bevel lightly on the wheel and adjust the jig in or out until the marker is removed off the entire face of the bevel. Continue grinding the gouge from side to side over the entire length of the bevel until it is sharpened. Both tools can also be ground to a side grind (see the following steps).

Sharpening a Side Grind on a Bowl Gouge or a Spindle Gouge

1

The spindle gouge on the top is ground with a side grind, or a "fingernail profile," and the bottom is a traditional grind of 35 degrees. A fingernail profile gives better tool control and overall ease of use with less chance of the sides of the gouge digging into the wood because the sides of the gouge are ground back so they cannot dig into the wood fibers. Bowl gouges can also be ground with a fingernail grind.

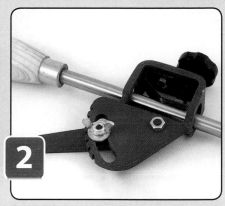

2

Sharpening a side grind (also known as the Ellsworth grind, Liam O'Neil, Irish grind, or a fingernail profile) on a bowl gouge or a spindle gouge is difficult to accomplish without some sort of jig since you have to complete a rolling and sweeping motion at the same time. An attachment, such as the Wolverine Vari-Grind attachment, will consistently produce sharp, repeatable bevels on your turning tools while shaping the modern side grind and the traditional fingernail shape for spindle work.

3

Secure the bowl gouge into the attachment and adjust the pocket of the grinding jig until the bevel just rubs the grinding wheel, as illustrated.

4

Turn on the grinder and make sure the attachment is firmly resting against the back pocket of the jig. Move the gouge from side to side in a sweeping motion, maintaining forward pressure at all times.

5

This is now grinding off the sides of the gouge in a uniform manner to produce the fingernail profile.

Skew Chisel – 60 degrees

1

2

3

Using the skew attachment with the sharpening system makes it easier to create a flat, consistent bevel. The design of this particular jig helps to eliminate the "hollow grind" associated with sharpening a skew on a grinding wheel.

Using a marker, mark the sides of the skew as you did with the roughing gouge. Place the skew into the left pocket of the attachment with the short point to the left. Line up the bevel, move the jig in or out to align the skew and the wheel, and start to grind a flat surface on one side. Move the skew back and forth using small side-to-side movements. When that side is completed, flip the skew over and place it into the right pocket with the short point to the right. Repeat the procedure.

The bevel of a skew should be flat with one continuous bevel.

It should never look like it has a multi-faceted edge.

Scraper Tool – 80 degrees

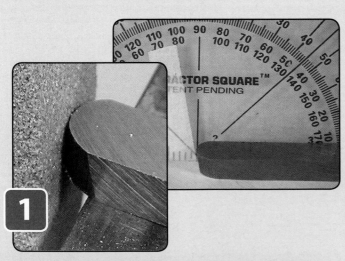

1

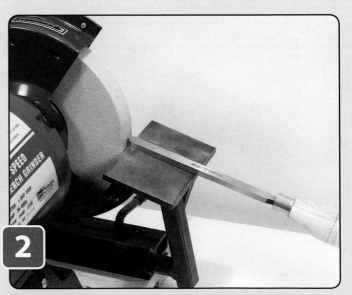

2

Set the angle of the platform to match the bevel of the scraper, approximately 80 degrees.

Turn the grinder on and move the scraper from side to side in a sweeping motion to sharpen the edge of the scraper.

Sanding

Like your sharpening equipment, you'll want to have sanding materials ready for when you finish your project. The objective here is not to turn you into a sandpaper master but to illustrate some of the alternative materials used for sanding and the techniques to best sand your particular project.

Let's be honest. No one likes to stand at the lathe for any length of time to sand a project. As you become more experienced with your turning tools (and you will), the less sanding you will have to do. However, as a beginner, sanding will be your new best friend when it comes to smoothing over an edge or removing a tool mark. Do not feel afraid to use a 60-grit sandpaper "gouge" to shape a project because your proficiency with a skew or a scraper has not yet been mastered. Numerous turning instructors would cringe at that last statement, but the truth is that many of us started out using sandpaper as a "gouge."

Why sand at all? Sanding should be completed to remove any tool marks or scratches that are present in the wood. In addition, it is the first step to a well-defined finish for your project. The two methods of sanding that turners use are power sanding, which is mostly for faceplate work, and hand sanding, which is primarily for spindle work.

All sandpaper is not created equal, and some of the more common sandpaper materials offered to turners are silicon carbide, aluminum oxide, and garnet sandpaper. These sandpaper types are offered to the general public as commercial grade or industrial grade. Industrial grade sandpaper is designed to withstand the harsh environment of factory/production work. It generally will have a heavier backing material, and the abrasive will be bonded by some sort of resin glue. Commercial grade sandpaper that is purchased at your local DIY outlet generally has a lighter backing material that is bonded to the abrasive by a glue other than industrial resin glue (see **Photo 1.50**).

Photo 1.50. Pictured from the lower left are cloth-backed aluminum oxide discs (green), New Wave Hi-Per Gold material attached to an angle sander, Abranet sanding screens, and Abralon foam pads.

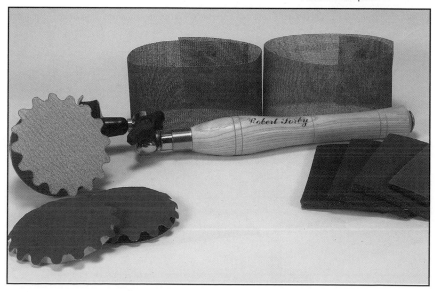

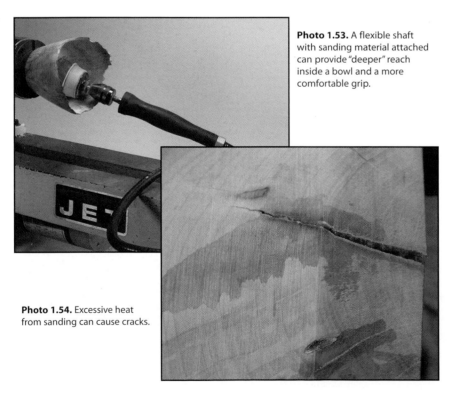

Photo 1.51. An angle sander's articulated head allows it to sand in a variety of angles, making it easy to sand the outside of a bowl.

Photo 1.52. Sanding pads chucked into a hand drill can also work well for power sanding.

Photo 1.53. A flexible shaft with sanding material attached can provide "deeper" reach inside a bowl and a more comfortable grip.

Photo 1.54. Excessive heat from sanding can cause cracks.

Method One: Power Sanding

Power Sanding Tools and Supplies

- Angle sander and flexible shaft
- Assorted grits of sanding material, 60 to 800 grit (New Wave sanding material was used for the demonstration)
- Sanding pads (Abralon sanding pads were used for the demonstration)

Power sanding is used in faceplate turning on larger objects to make the job of sanding a bit easier. An angle sander has an articulating head, which allows the head of the sanding pad to be placed at a variety of angles (see **Photo 1.51**). The sanding pad is driven by the force of the spinning work during the sanding process. Sanding near the outside edge of the bowl will cause the sander to spin faster; moving toward the center will make it spin slower.

Another way to power sand is to use sanding pads that are chucked into a hand drill (see **Photo 1.52**). The hand drill can be used in conjunction with the turning lathe. Because the drill will spin in the opposite direction of the lathe, this will speed up the sanding process. It will also increase the heat that is generated while sanding, which can cause cracks. If you do not have a hand drill, a flexible shaft chucked into your drill press can perform the same task as a hand drill. I find the flexible shaft is a bit more convenient and less strenuous to hold in my hand than the weight of a hand drill when I am sanding for long periods of time (see **Photo 1.53**).

Sanding Tip: Excessive heat will cause cracks in your work, so do not overheat the piece when sanding—especially if you're working with very thin turned bowls (see **Photo 1.54**).

Method Two: Hand Sanding

Hand Sanding Tools and Supplies

■ Assorted grits of sanding material, 60 to 800 grit (New Wave sanding material was used for the demonstration)

■ Sanding screens (Abranet screens were used for the demonstration)

■ Sanding pads (Abralon sanding pads were used for the demonstration)

Hand sanding is primarily used for spindle and smaller workpieces, but you can hand sand bowls as well. As the lathe spins, hold the sandpaper lightly against the piece that is to be sanded. When hand sanding, make sure that you sand in the six o'clock position with your dust extraction system in close proximity (see **Photo 1.55**). If you try to sand in the nine o'clock position or above, the sanding material will be thrown up in the air or at your face.

To keep an edge crisp and sharp on spindle work, it is easier to hand sand with a piece of sandpaper than it is to use a power sander. A small pad with sandpaper wrapped around it will facilitate sanding those hard-to-reach areas, such as beads and coves (see **Photo 1.56**).

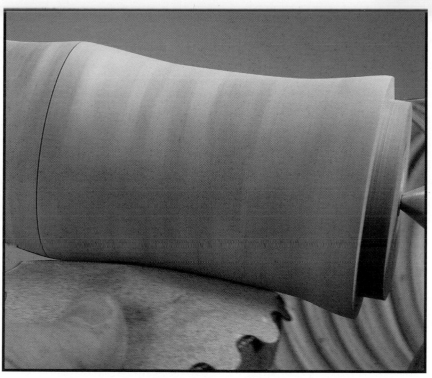

Photo 1.55. Hand sand in the six o'clock position to avoid getting dust in your face.

Photo 1.56. To assist your sanding efforts, use a pad that will conform to the coves. Any piece of soft material, such as part of a rubber mat, can be used as a sanding pad.

Photo 1.57. "Wavy" disks, such as these from New Wave, help to eliminate sharp edges from the insides of your bowls.

Photo 1.58. Notice how the wavy edges conform to the shape of the bowl, leaving a smoother finish.

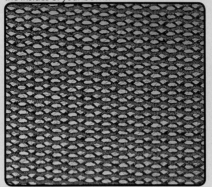

Photo 1.59. This sanding material, called Abranet, does not load up as frequently as normal sandpaper.

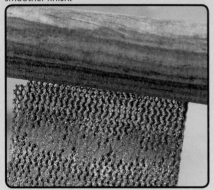

Photo 1.60. Sanding cocobolo creates dust and loads up normal sandpaper quickly.

Photo 1.61. To remove debris from the sanding material, simply "flick it" with your finger.

Photo 1.62. The maple burl bowl is being sanded with the sanding pad.

Photo 1.63. A sanding pad, such as this Abralon one, works to remove microscratches after the workpiece has been sanded up to 600 to 800 grit.

Photo 1.64. The shine on this piece was obtained with only the sanding pad. No finish was applied.

Alternative sanding materials

Some newer sanding materials, such as New Wave sanding discs, come in "wavy" discs with fingerlike edges that flex smoothly to assist in eliminating swirls and sharp-edge cuts on the insides of turnings (see **Photo 1.57**). These discs are ideal for bowl turners to eliminate the sharp edges left by standard circular sanding pads (see **Photo 1.58**). Note how the wavy edges fold over to meet the contour of the bowl to leave a smooth surface.

Screening material, such as Abranet sanding material, comes in assorted grits, and the key advantage to this sort of material is that it does not "load up" and can be cleaned with compressed air (see **Photo 1.59**). Cocobolo, for instance, is one of the worst woods when sanded. It will quickly load your sandpaper with debris (see **Photo 1.60**). This sanding material can be cleaned easily by blowing off the debris and continuing the sanding process (see **Photo 1.61**).

Some sanding pads, such as Abralon sanding pads, were specially designed sanding material for the solid surface industry and are used to polish countertops. However, this foam-backed material does an excellent job removing microscratches left by the typical sanding process. To use this material, sand as you normally would to 600 or 800 grit, and then use the sanding pads to finish your piece (see **Photo 1.62**). Notice the debris on the pad after the workpiece had been sanded with 800-grit sandpaper (see **Photo 1.63**). A beautiful shine can be coaxed from the wood with just the sanding pad and no finish (see **Photo 1.64**).

Remember, there is no right or wrong way to sand your piece. Whatever material you choose to use, make sure that you leave a scratch-free surface on which to apply your finish.

Finishing

Imagine spending hours creating a beautifully turned bowl from the most exotic burl in the world, and the finish you put on the bowl is not very good. In fact, it's horrible! Do not despair. As you obtain more experience applying finishes, your ability to put a good finish on your project will exponentially increase. All it takes is practice and a little common sense.

I was so proud of the first bowl I turned and finished. As I brought it to my woodturners' monthly club meeting, I noticed that, as the bowl was placed on the table, the other turned objects that were present had much better finishes on them. When I was asked to talk about my bowl, I informed the club members that my finish was just okay (as though they could not see that for themselves) and that I was looking for a perfect way to finish my work.

The group laughed at my "perfect finish" comment and said when I found it that I should sell it to them and every other turner in the world. It was then I realized that everyone has a different approach to finishing a project. Attend a monthly woodturners' meeting and ask ten of the attendees what type of finish they use and recommend, and you will get ten different answers. Remember, ways to finish a project are like fingerprints—everyone has one and each one is unique in its own presentation!

My approach to the perplexing topic of finishing is to keep it simple. There are hundreds of finishing products on the market today, and to review them all would take volumes of books, to

say the least. A few of the more popular types of finishes will be discussed over the next several pages, but the ultimate choice is yours, depending upon the results that you obtain from experimenting with these and other types of finishes.

Before choosing a finish, keep these few thoughts in mind:

- Where and how is your product ultimately being used? Is the piece you made a decorative piece or will it be used in and around food?

- How easy is the finish to apply? Do you want to use a spray, a brush, or a cloth to apply the finish to your project?

- Appearance and durability are another factor to consider. Do you want a very high gloss or satin appearance? Will your piece be handled a great deal? If so, is the finish scratch resistant?

- Tactile feel is important for the end product. How the product feels in your customers' hands will assist you in the sale of your creation. What does the finish feel like after it has been applied and has dried?

With the above questions as guidelines, let us plunge into the subject of finishing and find out a few answers and some easy methods for your first turnings that may just last a lifetime.

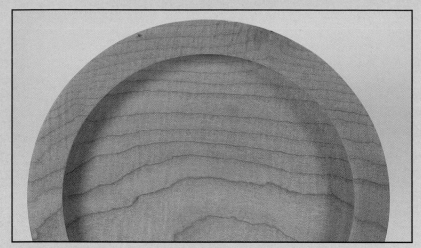

Photo 1.65. From a distance, this fiddleback maple bowl looks good.

Photo 1.66. Now, look at the same bowl with a single coat of salad bowl finish rubbed on it. Notice all of the scratches and end-grain tear-out. If the bowl were left as is, this would be a horrible finish.

Photo 1.67. Whether you are preparing for finishing or repairing a bad finish, the first step is to sand through 800 grit. Here I am using an Abralon sanding pad to prepare the surface for the finish.

Preparing the surface

First and foremost, before applying any finish, make sure that all tool marks, sanding scratches, end-grain tear-out, or any other minor defects are removed from the object to be finished. If a minor defect is present before the finish is applied, it will turn into a major defect as soon as that finish is placed on the piece (see **Photos 1.65** and **1.66**). To repair a bad finish, you must re-sand the bowl, starting at approximately 80 grit, and then continuing with the rest of the sanding process.

In final preparation before applying any finish, my recommendation is that sanding should be completed to at least 800 grit or by using sanding pads, such as Abralon ones (see **Photo 1.67**); then, use a tack rag or compressed air to remove any minor dust that may still be embedded in the grain of the wood. Completing this extra step will offer the best possible surface to which the finish can adhere.

Applying the different types of finish

Every finish has different characteristics and methods in which it can be applied. On the following pages, we'll look at a number of different finishes, what tools and supplies are needed for application, and what qualities each finish has.

Salad Bowl Finish

What you'll need:

- ■ Salad bowl finish
- ■ Lint-free cloth
- ■ 400-grit sandpaper or 4000-grit sanding pad

Photo 1.68. Salad bowl finish is a great non-toxic, food-safe finish.

Photo 1.69. Apply salad bowl finish with a lint-free cloth. To protect your hands, wear gloves when you are applying any finish.

Photo 1.70. Lightly sand between coats of salad bowl finish with a 4000-grit sanding pad, such as the Abralon one I'm using here.

Salad bowl finish is a good, safe, non-toxic product for any project that will come directly in contact with food, such as the bowl in **Photo 1.68**. Use this finish as the only finish on any wooden items that will come into contact with food. It leaves a tough, dry film that contains only food-safe ingredients. Once the final coat of salad bowl finish is applied, allow 72 hours before using the bowl with food to ensure that no lasting contaminants remain on the bowl.

Apply the finish with a lint-free cloth, rubbing the finish on and then wiping off any excess (see **Photo 1.69**). The manufacturer's instructions recommend six hours between coats; then, sand with 400-grit sandpaper and recoat. I usually wait 24 hours and then rub the piece with a 4000-grit sanding pad, like the Abralon one shown in **Photo 1.70**. The pad is less abrasive than 400-grit sandpaper and will not leave any visible scratches. In addition, several coats of salad bowl finish may be built up by simply rubbing the finish on with a lint-free cloth and then sanding between coats. Salad bowl finish is specially formulated with the application ease of an oil finish and the sheen-building properties and resistance of a varnish finish.

Tung Oil

What you'll need:
- ■ Tung oil
- ■ Mineral spirits
- ■ 400-grit sandpaper or 4000-grit sanding pad
- ■ Brush or lint-free cloth

 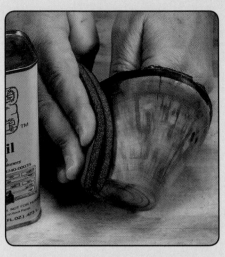 

Photo 1.71. Apply diluted tung oil with a rag and allow it to dry for 24 hours.

Photo 1.72. Lightly sand between coats of tung oil with a 4000-grit sanding pad, like the Abralon one I'm using here.

Photo 1.73. Apply extra tung oil to the bark to ensure that the bark stays on the bowl edge.

For many woodworkers, tung oil is their first choice because it is one of the most impervious and durable oil finishes. Some manufacturers, such as Behlen's, produce pure, unadulterated tung oil with no agents, such as varnishes or soy oils, added. The advantage of tung oil is a consistent quality finish that will build up to be extremely hard and durable, which means that it is resistant to water, stains, scratches, heat, and mildew. However, any imperfections can be easily buffed out with sanding pads and then retouched with tung oil if necessary. If you are using a manufacturer's pure tung oil, you will need to thin it with up to four parts mineral spirits to one part tung oil before application. This mixture will allow the oil to penetrate the wood to a greater depth.

Application is easy with tung oil (see **Photo 1.71**). You can apply it with a brush or just place some oil on a lint-free cloth and rub the piece, allowing the oil to soak into the wood while removing any excess. Allow 24 hours between coats and then use the appropriate sanding material to rub any "high" spots that might have popped up (see **Photo 1.72**).

Tip: When finishing natural-edge bowls, be sure to go over the edges a few times to allow some extra oil to penetrate the bark to aid in keeping the bark on the bowl's natural edge (see **Photo 1.73**).

Spray Lacquer

What you'll need:

■ Sanding sealer
■ Spray lacquer
■ 4000-grit sanding pad or 0000 steel wool

Photo1.74. Spray lacquer finish is best used in conjunction with sanding sealer.

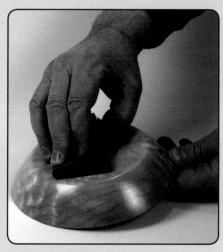

Photo 1.75. In between coats of sanding sealer and final finish, use a 4000-grit sanding pad, like this Abralon one, to remove any "wood fuzz" that might pop up.

Photo 1.76. Spray approximately 12" away from the piece and use a back and forth motion, applying many light coats.

Before spraying any lacquer finish (see **Photo 1.74**), make sure that the surface of the turned object is completely free of any dust or dirt and that you are spraying in a well-ventilated area. When spraying lacquer, it is important to apply a sanding sealer coat first. The sanding sealer fills the minute pores in the wood and causes the wood "fuzz" to stand up so it can be sanded smooth. Sanding sealer should be applied in two very thin coats at right angles to each other. By using sanding sealer in a crisscross fashion, you will get a hard, clear, strong, binding undercoat for the final spray lacquer finish to be applied. After each light coat, sand the piece with a 4000-grit sanding pad, such as an Abralon pad, or 0000 steel wool. The sanding pad is preferred since it will not leave behind the steel fibers as does the steel wool (see **Photo 1.75**).

Spray the lacquer finish approximately 12" away from the piece and spray in a back-and-forth motion, not staying in one area too long (see **Photo 1.76**). You will obtain the best results by taking the time, when you are spraying, to build up many thin coats rather than one thick one. After each light coat is dry, sand the surface of the piece smooth. If you try to spray the piece all in one coat, you are assured to have runs and drips on your piece. If this occurs, you will have to sand them off and start over!

Woodturner's Finish and EEE Cream

Photo 1.77. This type of finish is a two-step process using woodturner's finish and EEE polish.

Photo 1.78. Apply a small amount of EEE polish with your finger while the lathe is running at a medium speed (approximately 700 rpm).

Photo 1.79. Use cheese cloth to remove the excess EEE polish while allowing the heat to seal the polish into the wood.

My preferred method for smaller turned objects, such as pens, ornaments, small boxes, and other pieces 2" in diameter or less, is to use EEE Cream and woodturner's finish (see **Photo 1.77**) while the piece is still on the lathe. This method is fast and utilizes the speed of the lathe to assist you in placing a finish on the surface of the piece.

The first step, after the piece has been thoroughly sanded, is to use EEE Cream to seal the surface of the piece, to remove any microscratches that may still be visible, and to provide a luster to the piece. Put a small amount of cream on your finger and then apply this to the underside of the piece with the lathe speed at about 500 to 700 rpm to spread the cream all over the piece (see **Photo 1.78**). Make sure that you thoroughly cover the piece with this cream. Increase the speed of the lathe to 1500 to 2000 rpm and, using a soft, lint-free cloth or a piece of cheesecloth, apply some additional pressure to the piece. Allow the frictional heat to build up on your fingers; this is sealing and starting to polish the piece (see **Photo 1.79**). Continue for approximately 15 to 20 seconds with the heat building up, and then stop the lathe and allow the piece to cool down. This is the first step to a long-lasting shine on your project.

What you'll need:

■ EEE Cream
■ Woodturner's finish
■ Soft, lint-free cloth or piece of cheesecloth
■ Paper towels

Photo 1.80. Make sure that you hold onto the cheese cloth or this may happen to you!

Photo 1.81. Apply a small amount of woodturner's finish with a paper towel and allow friction to seal the lacquer finish to the workpiece.

Photo 1.82. The finished pieces have a rich, deep shine.

Caution: Do not let the loose end of the cheesecloth get tangled up in the spinning lathe (see **Photo 1.80**)!

The next step is to place some woodturner's finish on a paper towel and apply it on the piece with the lathe running slowly (see **Photo 1.81**). Gradually increase the speed to 1500 rpm while applying more pressure, which in turn is polishing the piece. You may repeat this step to add a deeper, richer shine, but quite often this is not necessary (see **Photo 1.82**). One coat will work just fine. After all, you are applying 1500 mini-coats of polish per minute if your lathe is set to 1500 rpm.

Photo 1.83. A buffing system, such as the Beal Buffing System, can be a fast, easy way to apply a beautiful finish.

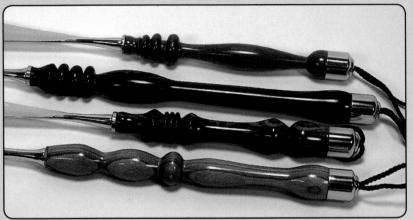

Photo 1.84. This spindle work was finished with either the woodturner's finish and EEE polish or the buffing system—can you tell the difference?

Photo 1.85. Here an old oil burner motor is used to drive the buffing system.

Photo 1.86. Apply tripoli compound to the wheel.

Buffing System

What you'll need:

- Buffing system
- Bowl buffs
- Tripoli buffing wheel
- Tripoli buffing compound
- White diamond wheel
- White diamond buffing compound
- Carnauba buffing wheel
- Carnauba wax

One of my favorite finishes is created with a buffing system (see **Photo 1.83**). In my humble opinion, this is a fast, easy way to apply a beautiful, tactile finish to any project in minutes. Can you tell which pieces were buffed and which received woodturner's finish in **Photo 1.84**? It is difficult to distinguish until the piece is picked up in your hands and touched, and then you can tell, by the soft feel of the carnauba wax, which one was buffed.

Buffing Tip: Trust me—this is a good one! Place a container of turned wood shavings directly underneath the buffing wheel to act as a cushion to catch your project when it is ripped from your hands. There is a great deal of downward thrust from the spinning motor, so having a container of shavings to catch your piece is a good idea; the ground is very hard and unforgiving. Notice the broken hollow vessel; if I had had the box in place as I was buffing the vessel, I could have avoided breaking it!

To begin the polishing process, the manufacturer recommends that you sand to 220 grit, but this turner prefers to sand to at least 800 grit and then seal the piece with a coat of diluted Tung oil or Watco oil for a more durable finish. When the oil is thoroughly dry, you may begin the polishing process. Some oily woods such as cocobolo, snakewood, and other South American woods have natural oils in the wood; therefore, coating them with more oil may not be necessary.

Any motor that turns a maximum of 1725 rpm can be utilized as a buffing motor. The motor pictured is an old oil burner motor that is mounted on a rolling stand (see **Photo 1.85**).

The first buffing wheel to be used is the tripoli rouge wheel. Apply some tripoli rouge to the wheel by lightly touching the rouge stick to the wheel as it is spinning; do not apply too much (see **Photo 1.86**). Securely hold your piece and let the wheel come in contact with the piece (see **Photo 1.87**). Apply the tripoli polish to the entire piece; both on the outside and on the inside of the bowl (see **Photo 1.88**).

Change to the next set of buffing wheels, which are the white diamond wheels, and apply the white diamond polish to the wheel and the bowl buff (see **Photo 1.89**). Buff the outside and the inside of the bowl as you did with the tripoli polish (see **Photo 1.90**).

The final step in the buffing process is carnauba wax. Change to the appropriate wheel and bowl buff and apply the carnauba wax to the wheel (see **Photo 1.91**). Polish the bowl with the carnauba wax using the same steps as described earlier (see **Photo 1.92**). Make sure you hold tight to the piece because the wax is slippery and the bowl may fly out of your hands. The end result of buffing is a beautifully finished bowl (see **Photo 1.93**).

Photo 1.87. Buff the outside of the bowl with tripoli rouge.

Photo 1.88. Use a bowl buff to apply the tripoli rouge to the inside of the bowl.

Photo 1.89. Apply the white diamond polish to the wheel.

Photo 1.90. Buff the inside of the bowl with the white diamond polish.

Photo 1.91. Apply the carnauba wax to the wheel.

Photo 1.92. Buff the bowl with the carnauba wax.

Photo 1.93. The bowl on the left was coated with tung oil, and the bowl on the right was coated with salad bowl finish. Both were then buffed with the buffing system.

Photo 1.94. Use dust extraction if you will be using a buffing system for extended periods of time.

Finishing safety

I would be remiss if I didn't include a few final notes on safety with respect to finishing.

■ When using a wipe-on finish of any sort, discard all dirty rags into metal containers. Do not leave them or discard them in areas with wood shavings. Spontaneous combustion is a serious issue that can happen with any old, oily rags that are left just lying around.

■ The spraying of a lacquer finish must be done in a well-ventilated area. Make sure that you keep the spray away from heat, sparks, or open flames.

■ When using a buffing system for long periods of time, wear both eye protection and a dust mask because of the silica quartz dust that is produced from the tripoli polish. This dust may cause temporary irritation to your eyes, nose, and respiratory tract, and excessive inhalation of the silica quartz dust may result in respiratory disease.

■ Also, place your vacuum system close to where you will be buffing your pieces to aid in removing some of the airborne particles (see **Photo 1.94**).

Start Turning

Now that you have chosen your lathe, transformed a log into turnable material, and sharpened your tools, it is time to put that knowledge to work! We are going to start with spindle turning to acquire some basic knowledge and skills, and then we'll graduate to more advanced turning, which will include faceplate turning.

Getting Ready to Turn

First, have it clear in your mind what type of turning you're about to do—spindle turning or faceplate turning. We'll start with spindle turning and then progress to faceplate turning.

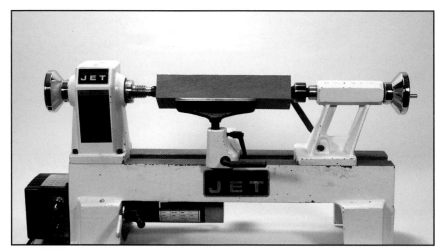

Photo 2.1. With spindle turning, the grain is running parallel to axis of the lathe.

Photo 2.2. In faceplate turning, the grain runs perpendicular to the lathe bed.

Spindle turning, or turning between centers, has the grain of the wood running parallel to the rotational axis of the lathe. In other words, the grain of the wood you are turning runs from the headstock to the tailstock (see **Photo 2.1**). When you are turning between centers you should always turn from the largest diameter to the smallest diameter, called turning "downhill," and you will be cutting with the grain, not against it as in faceplate turning.

Faceplate turning generally means that the grain is at 90 degrees to the axis of the lathe (see **Photo 2.2**). This means that for every revolution of the piece being turned, the end grain will be exposed twice. Objects being turned in faceplate turning will be held only at one end (headstock), but may be supported some of the time by bringing up the tailstock so that it comes in contact with the workpiece. Because the piece is being supported usually at only one end, a different set of rules will apply to faceplate turning than those that apply in spindle turning.

Mounting the workpiece

To mount a workpiece between centers, take a piece of wood at least 2" x 2" x 10" in length and mark the center of the wood by drawing a line from corner to corner on both ends of the wood (see **Photo 2.3**). Commercially available center finders also work well (see **Photo 2.4**).

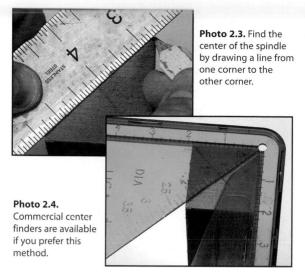

Photo 2.3. Find the center of the spindle by drawing a line from one corner to the other corner.

Photo 2.4. Commercial center finders are available if you prefer this method.

Photo 2.5. Lightly tap the drive spur into the center of the spindle.

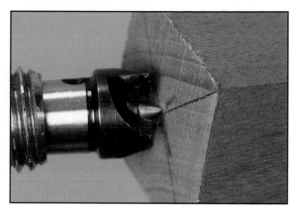

Photo 2.6. Replace the drive spur into the headstock and center the spindle into the center of the drive spur.

Rest the spindle on a hard surface and use a plastic or wooden mallet to tap the drive spur into the center of the spindle (see **Photo 2.5**). Remove the drive spur and place it into the headstock. Center the spindle blank onto the drive spur by placing it back into the holes you made previously by tapping the spur into the spindle blank (see **Photo 2.6**). Bring up the tailstock and continue turning the tailstock into the wood to ensure that the piece is firmly secured between the headstock and the tailstock.

Mounting your work for faceplate turning is different than mounting it between centers. You will use chucks or faceplates depending on the type of project you will be turning. We'll start with a spindle for practice; each of the faceplate turning projects will cover mounting the workpiece with the appropriate device.

Before you begin

There are a few points that you should familiarize yourself with concerning movement, balance, and stance before we start turning. It is critical for you to be comfortable in front of the lathe, so the way you stand in front of the lathe is important.

■ Remember that your feet should be comfortably spread apart, approximately shoulder-width, to offer optimal balance and movement. If you are not balanced on your feet, it will cause strain and fatigue, and that is when accidents happen.

■ Your elbows should be close to your body because your hips, shoulders, and elbows are a vital part in creating a comfortable stance in front of the lathe.

■ Try to relax. If you are too tense, that can cause fatigue as well. I know this may be the first time you are turning something, but this is a fun hobby, so enjoy it!

■ Before you turn on any lathe, make sure you check the speed of the lathe. When first starting to rough out a blank, the speed should be slow, about 500 to 700 rpm, until the workpiece is balanced. Then, the speed may be increased.

■ Turn the hand brake to ensure that the piece is not going to hit the tool rest, and make sure that all locking handles have been tightened.

■ Have your eye and dust protection ready to wear. You are now ready to turn!

The ABC's of tool control

Now that we're set up at the lathe, let's learn some techniques for using our tools. The ABC's described here are known as bevel cutting. You will obtain a dramatically smoother and better cut by letting the bevel rub against the surface of the material rather than by "scraping" the material. We will put these principles into practice in the next few pages.

Photo 2.7. Make sure the tool is resting securely on the tool rest.

The "A" Stands for Anchor.

When you are standing in front of the lathe with it running, make certain that your turning tool is firmly placed on the tool rest before contact is made with the wood (see **Photo 2.7**). Failure to secure the tool upon the tool rest prior to making contact with the wood will have a detrimental effect on you and your turning blank.

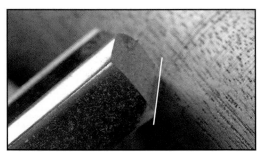

Photo 2.8. Make sure that only the lower portion of the bevel of the gouge is touching the surface.

The "B" Stands for Bevel.

Confirm that only the lower portion of the bevel touches the surface of the material before you start your cutting (see **Photo 2.8**). If this does not occur, you will get an immediate "dig-in" and, once again, possibly ruin your turning blank.

Photo 2.9. End grain tear-out, shown here, is caused by not riding the bevel of the bowl gouge.

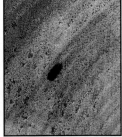

Photo 2.10. End grain tear-out can be reduced, if not eliminated, by riding the bevel of the bowl gouge.

The "C" Stands for Cut.

Once the tool is anchored and only the bevel of the tool is touching the surface, slowly raise the handle of the tool to engage the surface and proceed cutting your blank.

If the bevel of the gouge is supported by the wood, you will slice through the fibers of the wood rather than scraping them, which would cause some tear-out of the fibers (see **Photo 2.9**). If the proper bevel-rubbing technique is followed, the tear-out is greatly reduced, if not eliminated (see **Photo 2.10**).

Tool holding techniques

There are two main ways to hold the turning tool. The first is the "underhand" technique of holding the tool (see **Photo 2.11**). Note that the thumb is positioned so it can lightly hold down the top of the tool while your fingers support the tool from the bottom. Meanwhile, your other hand is holding the back of the tool, waiting until you slowly raise the tool in order to make contact with the turning blank and start your cutting action. This technique can be done with either your left or your right hand.

There is also an "overhand" technique (see **Photo 2.12**). The front hand is firmly holding the tool down against the tool rest, while the back hand is holding the tool and waiting to raise it up in order to make contact with the material. This overhand technique is primarily used for larger turned objects; the underhand technique is most widely used for smaller objects and finishing cuts.

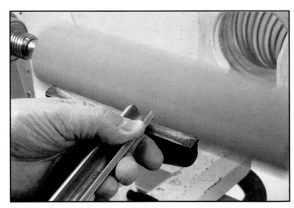

Photo 2.11. With the underhand tool grip, the thumb holds down the gouge.

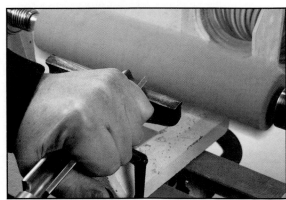

Photo 2.12. With the overhand tool grip, the front hand holds the tool against the tool rest.

Tool rest position

Turn the hand brake and make sure that the turning material does not hit the tool rest. Position the tool rest with approximately ⅛" space in between the material and the tool rest (see **Photo 2.13**). If the space between the material and the tool rest is too wide, the turning tool can get caught and be ripped right out of your hand (see **Photo 2.14**).

The height of the tool rest is critical, especially since you want to cut the surface of the wood with the best possible results. The tool rest should be in a position equal to the center of the workpiece when the tool you choose is placed on the tool rest (see **Photo 2.15**). Here the cutting edge of the gouge is in the centerline of the workpiece when placed on the tool rest.

Making the first cut

With the ABC's, tool gripping techniques, and tool rest position and height out of the way, we can start with the first tool to use in spindle turning, which is the roughing-out gouge, or roughing gouge. Grasp the gouge with an overhand technique, place the gouge securely on the tool rest, and lower the handle of the gouge so the lower portion of the bevel of the gouge comes into slight contact with the wood. Start to raise the handle, holding it close to your body, and...wow, you are cutting your first piece of wood with a roughing gouge (see **Photo 2.16**)!

If the material you use is very dry, the pieces being chipped off are hot and may sting your hand, so a glove may be worn for comfort. Continue to go back and forth until the piece is round. Once it is round, increase the speed of the lathe and take a final, very light pass over the entire piece with just the bevel rubbing the wood (see **Photo 2.17**). Note the fine shavings that are produced if the bevel is just lightly cutting the fibers of the wood.

Photo 2.13. The tool rest should be approximately ⅛" away from the spindle.

Photo 2.14. If the tool rest is not close to the workpiece, a catch can tear the tool from your hand.

Photo 2.15. The tool rest height should be approximately in the center of the spindle.

Photo 2.16. The gouge lightly removes the sharp edges of the blank.

Photo 2.17. Ride the bevel of the roughing gouge to smooth the cutting action of the tool.

Turning Tool Exercises

Now that you have your workpiece mounted and you've practiced a little bit of turning, let's look at what some of the turning tools can do.

Roughing Gouge

For the roughing gouge, we will learn how to form coves on our workpiece. Forming coves with the roughing gouge is easy because you will use the radius of the tool to form the cove. The roughing gouge's primary functions are turning blanks from square to round and forming coves.

1

To start the cove, turn the roughing gouge up on its side and let the bevel rub against the wood.

2

Now, let the bevel rub and lift your back hand and start to cut the wood; at the same time, roll the gouge upward toward the ceiling. At the end of the cut you should be in the center of the cove with the gouge facing up.

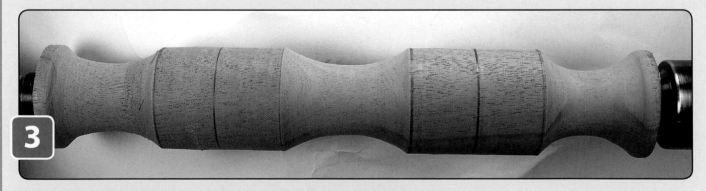

3

Practice these gouge moves on the rest of the piece, and your piece should look similar to the one shown here. Don't worry if they did not turn out quite right. Just get the movement and feel of the tool, and, with time, they will improve.

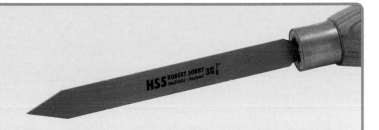

Parting Tool

Another tool you will use will be the parting tool. The parting tool is used primarily for parting off pieces, but it can be used in other ways, such as making feathering cuts, turning small beads, and making sizing cuts.

1

Measure 1" increments and mark them with a pencil, as shown.

2

Next, use the parting tool to cut a groove into the wood to divide your work into sections. Did you remember your ABC's? To correctly use the parting tool, rest it on the tool rest (A), then let the bevel of the tool come in contact with the wood fibers (B), and then start to lift the handle to cut the wood (C).

Spindle Gouge

The spindle gouge is used to make beads, coves, and other decorative items.

1

On the wood you marked, divide the 1" marks into ½" marks and remove the wood in between the marks to 1½" in diameter.

2

Place the spindle gouge on the tool rest with the flute facing up and drop the hand holding the tool, which will raise the bevel of the gouge to come into contact with the wood.

3

Taking small bites, start to roll the gouge while maintaining the bevel rubbing against the wood.

4

You should end your rolling motion with the gouge facing the inside of the wood. The bevel should always be riding the wood.

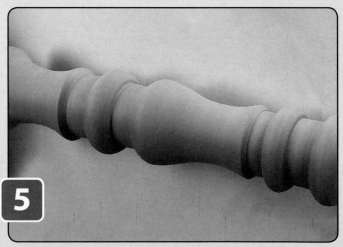

5

This is the end product of several beads and coves with a little extra thrown in.

Skew

Once mastered, the skew will be your favorite tool. It leaves a wonderfully smooth finish on your work, and it can perform other tasks, such as turning beads. The skew should be used similar to any other turning tool.

1

2

Make sure that the tool is anchored on the tool rest, and then let the bevel of the skew rub against the wood. Lift your hand holding the handle to start the cutting action. Use the long point of your skew to mark off ⅜" sections on your wood.

Tip: If the tip of the skew does not have support, then a catch will occur similar to the one shown.

Rub the bevel of the skew against the wood and slowly roll the skew into the cut you made, using the heel of the tool. Keep in mind that you should follow the bevel of the skew so you will not have a catch.

3

Your finished beads should look something like this. The more you practice with a skew, the better you will become. However, if you cannot get the hang of it, you can try using the Spindlemaster (see page 50) to complete this exercise.

Spindlemaster

One of the best tools for spindle work is the skew; but, since many beginners have trouble with the skew, we will learn to use the Spindlemaster to get the same motion and cuts as you would using the skew. The Spindlemaster is a combination of a skew and a spindle gouge, but it is much easier to use than a skew and gives a very smooth finish. Anything that a spindle gouge or a skew does, the Spindlemaster can perform without the fear of a catch.

Reduce another 2" x 2" x 10" piece of wood using the roughing gouge. Notice how rough the wood is after using only the roughing gouge.

The Spindlemaster left a smoother finish than the roughing gouge did.

Notice the section of wood on the left was cut by the roughing gouge and the section on the right was cut with a single pass of the Spindlemaster.

Spindle Turning Projects

Now that you have practiced working with your tools, it's time to put your hard work into action by making a few projects that will solidify your skills. You can create many nice projects working between centers (spindle turning), and the following projects will test your skills while making some very functional gifts for family and friends. The projects are ordered from the easiest to the more difficult so that you can build skills as you progress through the projects.

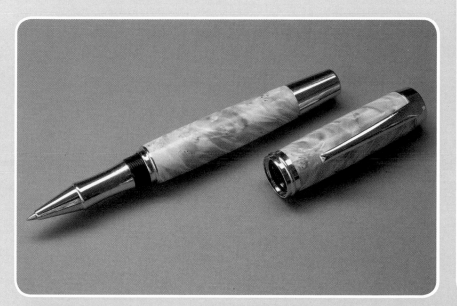

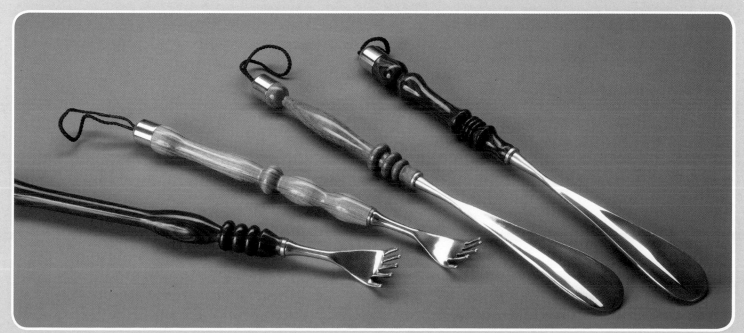

Back Scratcher or Shoehorn

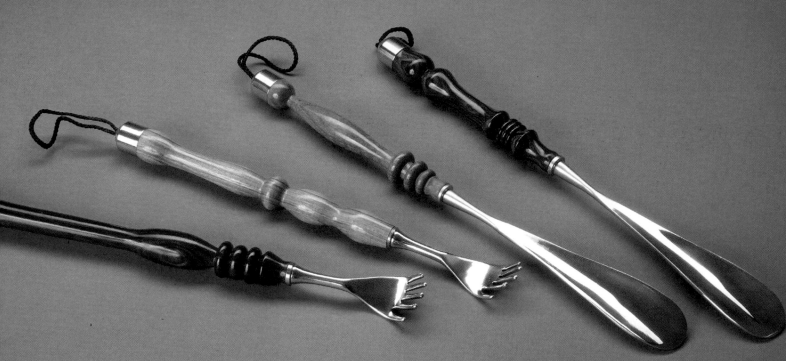

From top to bottom: cocobolo shoehorn, tulipwood shoehorn, pink ivory back scratcher, and cocobolo back scratcher.

We all have a relative that may be horizontally challenged or would rather not bend over to put their shoes on; a long-handled shoehorn will make life a lot easier for those family members. And who amongst us has never rubbed their back on a corner of a wall and wished we had a back scratcher? Using the same turning techniques, you can accessorize this project with your choice of a back scratcher or shoehorn kit.

Tools and Supplies

- **Roughing gouge**
- **Spindlemaster or skew**
- **Parting tool**
- **Digital or regular calipers**
- **Wood of choice (1½" x 1½" x 12" long)**
- **Sanding material**
- **Back scratcher or shoehorn kit**
- **²³⁄₆₄"drill bit for the back scratcher/shoehorn front end**
- **CA glue**
- **Finish of choice (EEE Cream, woodturner's finish)**
- **Lathe (speed set to 500 to 2000 rpm)**

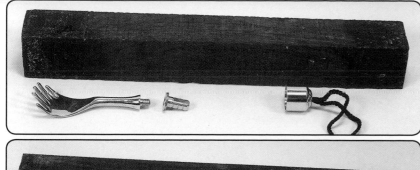

1 Familiarize yourself with the different pieces of the kit by lining up the parts and the 12"-long square stock you have selected.

2 Mark the center of the wood by drawing a line from corner to corner on both ends of the wood. Tap the drive spur with a plastic or wooden mallet into the center of the spindle. Mount the stock between centers.

3 Reduce the square stock to a cylinder with a roughing gouge. A replaceable-tip tool, such as the New Edge ½" round scraper, will also work.

4 Smooth the cylinder with a Spindlemaster or a skew in the bevel-rubbing mode. Notice the clean shavings coming off the "sweet spot" of the skew (see inset photo).

5 Compare the surface of the wood turned with just the roughing gouge on the left to the wood turned with the skew or Spindlemaster on the right.

6 Use a parting tool to make a sizing cut down to approximately ⅞" thick on both ends of the spindle.

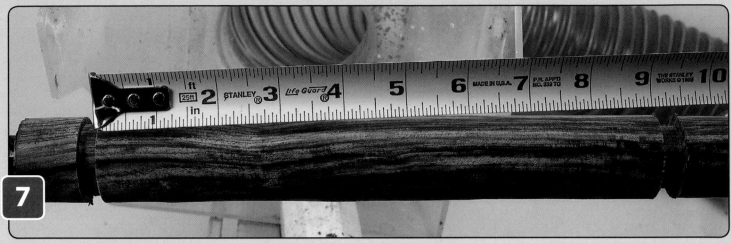

7

The back scratcher should be approximately 9" in length and the shoehorn 7" in length.

8

Use calipers to make sure that the sizing cuts are all the same diameter.

9

Use a skew or a Spindlemaster to reduce the cylinder down to the sizing cut as noted by the arrow.

10 Measure the inside diameter of the end cap with calipers.

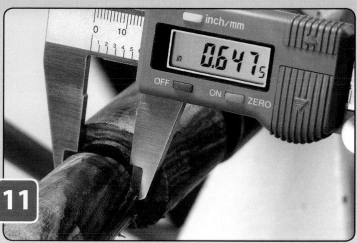

11 Use that same measurement and reduce one end of the cylinder to match the inside diameter of the end cap.

12 At the other end of the cylinder, start to create some beads, coves, lines, or any other ornamental decorations of your choosing.

13 Using a skew or the Spindlemaster with the flat edge facing up, rub the bevel against the wood and start to roll it to the right, ending with the flat edge on its side. Make sure that the bevel is rubbing against the wood the entire time. Continue completing the rest of the beads.

14 Since we are still learning, if the beads are not perfect, you can use sandpaper to make them look nice. When you finish, no one will ever know how you made those beads—unless you tell them!

15 Continue sanding with all of the grits from 100 to 800 and then use sanding pads, such as this Abralon one, to remove any microscratches. Finish the piece using the EEE Cream and woodturner's finish, as illustrated in the finishing section on page 36, or using the finish of your choice.

16

Use a parting tool, reducing both ends a little at a time but leaving a small connection to the headstock end.

17

Use a parting tool with one hand; use your other hand to catch the piece as you part it away from the tailstock end.

18

Place the back end into a four-jawed chuck, and, using a Jacobs Chuck with a 23/64" drill bit, drill a hole into the opposite end to accommodate the scratcher end of the back scratcher or the horn end of the shoehorn.

19

Use a small spindle gouge to remove the nub from the end of the spindle, and glue the brass end onto the scratcher using a medium grade of CA glue.

20

Here are your finished back scratchers and shoehorns.

Spindle Turning
Peppermill

Tools and Supplies

- Roughing gouge
- Spindlemaster or skew
- Parting tool
- Wood of choice (curly sapele 3" x 3" x 11" long)
- Sanding material
- Peppermill kit (10")
- Four-jawed chuck and cone center
- Jacobs Chuck
- Thin-bladed back saw
- Forstner bits, ½", 1", 1⅝"
- Salad bowl finish
- Lathe (speed set to 500 to 2000 rpm)
- Tailstock with a cone center

A peppermill is a useful and sensible kitchen utensil that everyone can use, and a handmade peppermill is an especially nice gift. Peppermills are easy and fun to make. The shape of a peppermill is as varied as the imagination of the maker of the piece. When designing a peppermill, roughly 70 percent should be the general length of the body, and the top should be no more than 30 percent of the overall length. Peppermill grinding mechanisms are generally 6", 8", 10", and 12" in length, and, when choosing a mechanism, an additional 1" to 2" in length of wood is necessary to turn the piece. Another thought to keep in mind when choosing a peppermill kit is the length of the grinding mechanism. It is difficult to turn a 12" grinding mechanism on a mini-lathe when you are restricted to an overall length of 14" between centers.

1 Reduce the 3" x 12" square stock to a cylinder using a roughing gouge; the surface should be flat. A replaceable-tip tool, such as the New Edge ½" round scraper, will work also.

2 Use a parting tool to square both ends of the cylinder. You should get clean shavings from your parting tool, as illustrated.

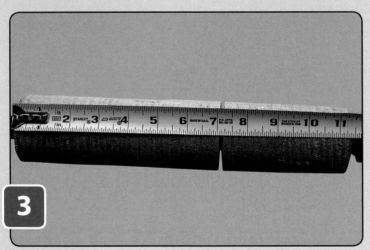

3 Lay out the body and the top of the peppermill using a 70% (body) to 30% (top) rule.

4 Cut the cylinder using a thin parting tool. Cut down to about ⅝", being careful not to cut all the way through the cylinder. If you try to do this, the parting tool will bind up, and it will cause you extreme anxiety.

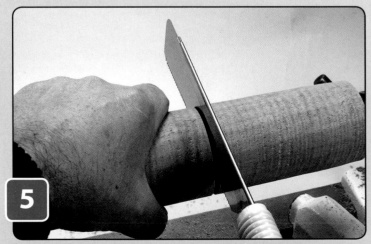

5 Finish cutting the piece into two sections with a thin-bladed back saw. Do not attempt to cut the piece with the lathe running!

6 Mount the lower portion of the body in a four-jawed chuck and, using a Jacobs Chuck with a 1⅝" Forstner bit, drill a hole ⅜" deep into the bottom of the body to hold the grinder mechanism.

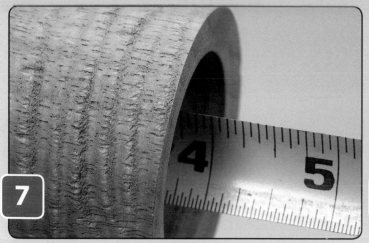

7

Now install a drill bit 1" in diameter and drill at least one-half of the length of the body. Then, turn the body around and mount it into the four-jawed chuck and drill the other half. If you try to drill the entire length, the drill bit will "wander" from center due to the grain of the wood.

8

Take the body of the peppermill out of the four-jawed chuck and reverse it again so the bottom of the mill is facing the tailstock that has been fitted with a cone center.

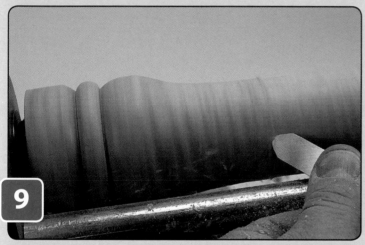

9

Use a skew or a Spindlemaster to generally shape your peppermill and add a bead or two on the bottom of the mill. Remove this from the lathe and set it aside for now.

10

Mount the top into the four-jawed chuck and drill a ¼" hole about halfway into the one end and again reverse the top and drill the other half of the ¼" hole in the top. This will ensure that the hole is centered in the top.

11

Turn a 1" spigot into the top end cap. Use the top half of the body of the peppermill as a guide to ensure a snug fit between the top and bottom sections of the peppermill.

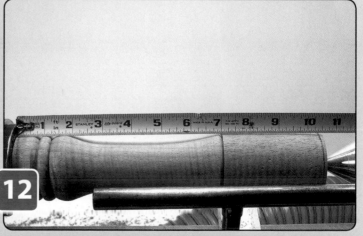

12

Place the two halves together and measure where the 10" will fall on the top portion of the peppermill. At this time, turn the top portion of the mill to the desired shape and length—remember, nothing too fancy, just keep it simple.

13

Place the top into the four-jawed chuck and refine the shape as necessary.

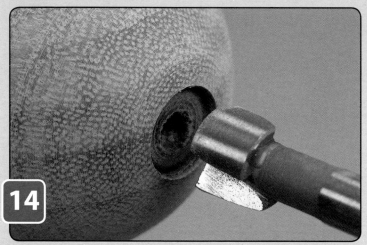

14

Use a ½" Forstner bit to drill the top to a depth of ⅛" to accommodate the top nut on the grinding mechanism to recess into the top.

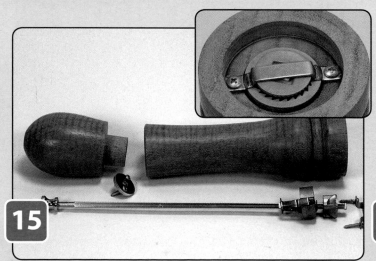

15

Finish the peppermill with a few coats of salad bowl finish and allow it to dry. Line up all of the pieces according to the manufacturer's instructions. Pre-drill the holes for the screws that hold the mechanism in place to avoid splitting the wood (inset).

16

Here is your finished peppermill.

Spindle Turning
Pen

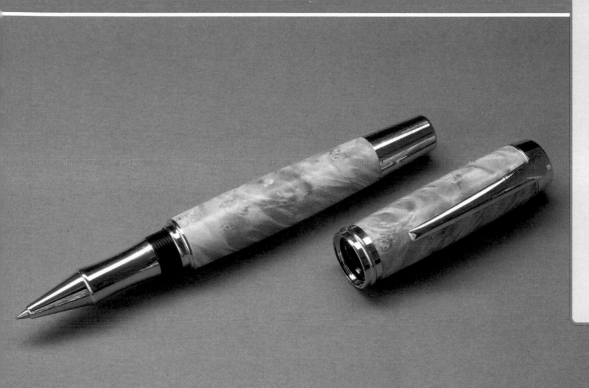

Tools and Supplies

- Roughing gouge
- Spindlemaster or skew
- Drill center
- Barrel trimmer
- Pen insertion tool
- Pen mandrel
- Pen press
- Pen kit of choice
- CA glue and accelerator
- Pen blank of choice
- EEE Cream
- Woodturner's finish
- Sanding pads
- Lathe (speed set to 1000 to 2500 rpm)

In these times of instant gratification, nothing satisfies a woodturner more than finishing a project in a few hours. Creating a fine writing instrument from a block of wood fits this mind-set. The styles, designs, and finishes for pen kits today have come a long way in just a few short years. Pen making appeals to a great number of people and has seen resurgence in popularity due to the short time needed to finish a project. Besides, don't we all need a pen or pencil to write with? And what better gift to give than a handmade writing instrument.

There are many styles of pens that are offered today, from the basic slimline to the elegant statesman's pen manufactured from rhodium-plated components (a platinum derivative) and 22K gold. Other quality pen kit manufacturers use rose gold and sterling silver as components for their kits. The pen kit chosen for this project is the Craft Supply Gentleman's Platinum Rollerball, and the pen blank is gold-dyed stabilized box elder burl.

You can use full-size turning tools, like the Spindlemaster on top, to make a pen; however, using tools more suited for smaller pieces, like the five bottom tools, will make your job easier.

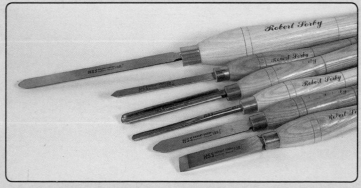

1

2

Remove the parts from the kit and read the instructions that came with the kit to understand how the project will be turned. Line up the pen mandrel, pen bushings, pen blank, and pen kit and familiarize yourself with the parts.

Use the pen tubes as a guide to cut the pen blank into two pieces slightly larger than the pen tubes. Rough up the surface of the tubes by scratching them on a piece of sandpaper so the tube can adhere better to the inside surface of the pen blank.

3

4

Use a drill-centering device and drill the pen blank with the appropriate size drill bit for the particular pen kit chosen.

Glue the pen tubes into the wooden pen blanks with a medium grade CA glue. Use a pen insertion tool so glue will not get on your fingers.

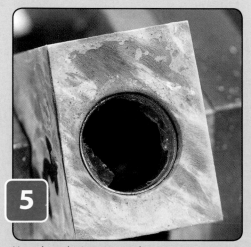

5

Use a barrel-trimming tool to remove any excess glue that was inside the tube and to ensure that the pen tube is now square to the pen blank.

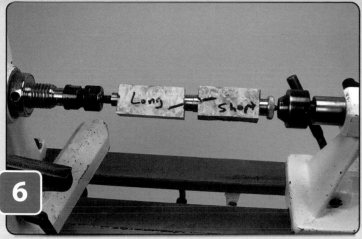

6

Position the mandrel into the headstock of the lathe, and then place the pen blanks onto the mandrel with the bushings for the Gentleman's pen in the correct orientation. Note the orientation marks on the pen blank.

7

Thread the locking nut on the mandrel; it should only be hand-tight! **Caution:** Make sure that you do not over-tighten the locking nut. If you do, damage to the mandrel may occur and your pen will not turn symmetrically. At this time, bring the tailstock up to the mandrel and lock it down. Also, do not place too much pressure on the mandrel from the tailstock.

8

Using a roughing gouge and the bevel-rubbing technique, have the gouge lightly touch the pen blank and move it back and forth along the blank to round the pen blank.

9

Use a skew to shape the pen blank. Notice the clean shavings coming off the sweet spot of the skew. If you cannot use a skew, use the Spindlemaster (see inset). Leave the pen blanks slightly proud of (slightly higher than) the bushings. Do not shape them flush with the bushings at this time.

10

The sanding grit that you will start with will depend on whether or not your pen blank has any tool marks or deep scratches. Usually, if you have used the skew or the Spindlemaster correctly, you can start out at 180- to 220-grit sandpaper.

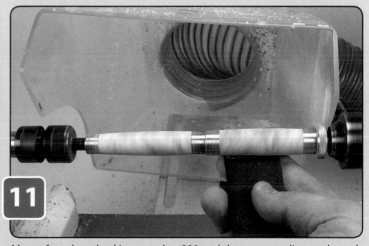

11

My preferred method is to sand to 800 and then use sanding pads, such as the Abralon sanding pads, to remove any microscratches and to offer the best possible surface for the finish. The pen blank should now be flush with the bushings.

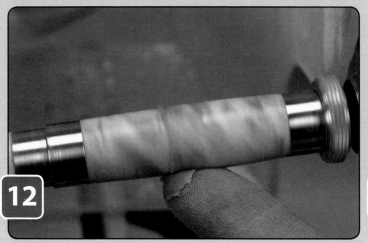

12 Apply a small amount of EEE Cream on your finger; then apply it to the workpiece with the lathe running at approximately 500 to 700 rpm.

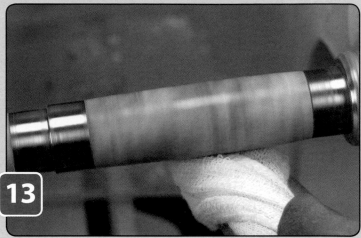

13 Turn up the speed of the lathe and apply pressure with a cheesecloth to build up some friction, thus sealing the EEE Cream into the pen blank.

14 Apply woodturner's finish to a paper towel and, with the lathe running, slowly apply the finish to the entire pen. Then, turn up the speed of the lathe and apply pressure to once again cause some friction to seal the polish into the pen.

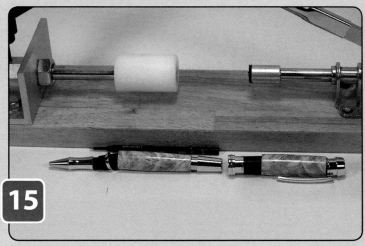

15 Arrange the finished pieces of the pen according to the assembly instructions for the pen.

16 Using a pen press, press the front end coupler and the end cap into the lower portion of the barrel as per the instructions for the pen kit and continue assembling the pen to completion.

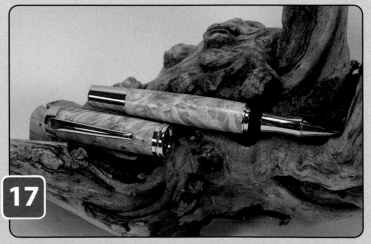

17 Here is your finished pen.

Faceplate Turning Projects

The objects that are being turned within this group are attached to the headstock with a four-jawed chuck, a screw chuck, or a faceplate. Most of the time, the object being turned is not supported by the tailstock and is just supported by the headstock. This group will include bowls, platters, boxes, and end grain vessels. The projects in this section are designed to take you from the easiest project (simple bowl) to the more difficult one (end-grain hollow vessel) while having fun, building confidence, and obtaining certain skill sets along the way. Sit back, have fun, and relax as you learn to turn using the faceplate method.

Faceplate Turning
Simple Bowl

Tools and Supplies

- ½" bowl gouge with fingernail profile
- Curved scraper and round nose scraper
- Four-jawed chuck and mini-jumbo jaws
- Faceplate and 1¼" square drive screws
- Double-ended calipers
- Dividers or compass
- Sanding pads and sandpaper in assorted grits
- Wood of choice (ambrosia maple, 8" in diameter x 4" thick)
- Lathe (speed set to 500 to 1500 rpm)
- Finish (salad bowl finish)

Because this is a simple bowl, do yourself a favor and use a simple, gradual shape for your bowl as indicated. When you gain more experience, you can be as creative as you want to be. But for your first bowl, keep it simple!

Bowl Safety Tip

When first starting your unbalanced bowl blank, bring up the tailstock to support the blank. A good habit is to use the tailstock as much as possible to support your work when turning.

Curved scraper and round nose scraper

Four-jawed chuck and mini-jumbo jaws

Double-ended calipers

1

Find the center of the bowl blank and mount a faceplate to it using 1¼" square drive screws.

2

Attach the faceplate to the headstock and bring up the tailstock as support for the unbalanced bowl blank. Rotate the hand brake to ensure that the blank does not strike the tool rest. The lathe speed should be the minimum, or approximately 500 rpm.

3

Starting at the tailstock and working forward toward the headstock using a ½" bowl gouge, take very small bites to get the blank as balanced as you can.

4

True up the face of the blank (make it level) and create a spigot for the four-jawed chuck. Note the nice clean shavings coming off the bowl blank because the tool is cutting in the bevel-rubbing mode.

5

Starting at the edge of the blank and cutting from the back to the front all in one motion to avoid a stepped surface, continue the gradual shaping of the bowl.

6

A divider set is used to mark the appropriate width for the four-jawed chuck. Make sure that the right side of the divider does not come in contact with the spinning bowl.

7

Using a bowl gouge, reduce the diameter of the spigot so it will fit into the chuck.

8

If the shape of the bowl is to your satisfaction, sand the blank at this time with a power sander, removing all tool marks and scratches. Do not be afraid to use more aggressive sandpaper if you still have tool marks in your bowl. Sandpaper can be your best way to remove unwanted tool marks.

9

Once all of the tool marks and scratches are removed, use sanding pads, such as Abralon pad, as the final sanding step.

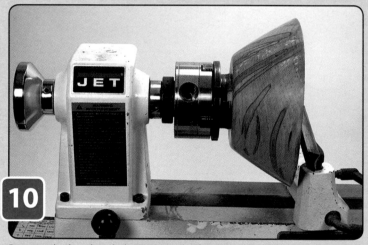

10

Reverse the bowl and place it into the four-jawed chuck.

11

Starting at the edge of the bowl and working toward the center, make sure that the bevel of the bowl gouge is parallel to the surface of the bowl. In addition, the wall thickness should be established at this point. Remember, we are just beginning, so the wall thickness does not have to be razor thin.

12

With the lathe turned off, you can see how the gouge is positioned to start cutting toward the center.

13 Continue cutting with the bevel rubbing all the way toward the center of the bowl. Practice making one pass from the beginning of the cut to the end to ensure a smooth surface inside the bowl.

14 The wall thickness should be checked at this point using double-ended calipers to make certain that a uniform thickness is maintained. Remove approximately 1" of wall material at a time so the fibers of the wood are always supported by the ones below it. Removing too much wall material from the inside at any given time makes it more difficult to maintain a smooth interior.

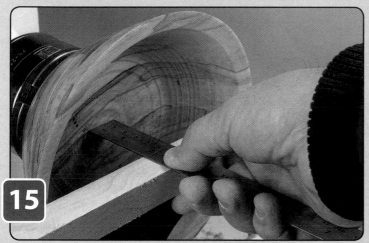

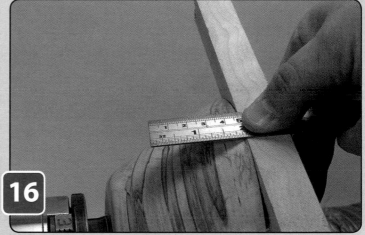

15 Take any flat edge and place it across the face of the bowl. Use a ruler to measure the depth of the bowl.

16 Transfer the flat edge to the top of the bowl to see how much more material you need to remove.

17 When the correct depth is obtained, use a round nose scraper to remove the nub left at the bottom of the bowl. Make sure that the bottom of the bowl is flat and does not have any bumps or ridges. Remember, when using any scraper, you must be slightly above the centerline of the bowl.

18 Power sand the inside of the bowl, making sure that your dust extraction system is near.

19 I chose the wavy sanding discs from New Wave because the waves on the disc conform to the inside of the bowl and do not leave scratch lines.

20 Finally, sand the inside of the bowl using sanding pads, such as the Abralon pad, to remove any microscratches and to offer the best possible surface for the finish.

21 For beginners, Oneway offers a revolving center that has an adapter so the bowl can be transferred from a four-jawed chuck to mini-jumbo jaws to reverse chuck the bowl, ensuring that the bowl is perfectly aligned and will run absolutely true.

22 The bowl is being held in place by the mini-jumbo jaws so the bottom of the bowl can be turned.

23 Remove the spigot from the bottom with a small bowl gouge, taking small bites each time.

24 Place a straight edge across the bottom of the bowl and make certain that there is a slight concave surface.

25

Add a little decoration, such as lines or small coves, to the bottom of the bowl.

26

Do not forget to sign your work.

27

Because this is a bowl that will come into contact with food, apply a coat of salad bowl finish.

28

Once the bowl has dried, use a 4000-grit sanding pad, like this Abralon one, to lightly sand the bowl, and apply another coat of salad bowl finish.

The finished bowl.

29

Faceplate Turning
Ornamental Birdhouse

Tools and Supplies

- Wood of your choice (preferably exotic woods, light in color, 1½" x 1½" x 2½" long)
- Roughing gouge
- Skew or Spindlemaster
- Spindle gouge
- Parting tool
- Digital calipers
- ½" and 1¼" Forstner bits, ⅛"drill bit
- Sandpaper, assorted grits up to 800 and sanding pads
- Woodturner's finish
- Stains (blood red, sea blue, and lemon yellow)
- Black marker or black acrylic paint (for inside of ornament)
- EEE Cream
- ⅞" thin eye pin for top of ornament
- CA glue (medium viscosity)
- Lathe (speed set to 1000 to 2000 rpm)

Use your own creativity to create other combinations using other exotic woods. Here are a few examples.

All of the woods used for these ornaments are light in color, so the stain will make the grain stand out. For this project, we'll be taking a highly figured piece of tiger-striped or bird's-eye maple and artificially injecting another color into the grain pattern. In addition, the pieces of wood were all taken from the scrap pile, which is why they are fun and profitable to make. For this ornament, lemon yellow and sea blue were mixed to create a green stain for the main body of the ornament. All of the other parts of the ornament used a contrasting blood-red stain for the roof, base, and perch to create a visually pleasing one-of-a-kind ornament.

For turned ornaments, a stain that is highly fade resistant and quick drying is important. Also, the capability to be ultraviolet resistant and non-grain raising are important attributes. Because the stain being used is an alcohol-based stain, it will not raise the grain after the ornament has been sanded. If you do not want to stain the ornament, you can finish it as indicated and leave the natural beauty of the wood to shine.

A word of caution when using stains or dyes: Avoid absorbing the dye through your skin by wearing protective gloves when working with these dyes; they will stain your hands if protection is not worn. Make sure adequate ventilation is present and wear a mask. To avoid the possibility of spontaneous combustion, discard the application rag outside in a metal container.

1

Cut the wooden blanks from lighter-colored, assorted exotic hardwoods to 1½" square and 2½" long.

2

Mark the center of the blank by drawing lines from corner to corner.

3

Drill the X-marked wooden blank using a drilling vise with a 1¼" Forstner bit. The drilling vise is used to ensure a straight bore directly through the center of the wooden blank.

4

Prepare a jam chuck 1¼" in diameter by mounting a block of wood 2" x 2" x 6" into a four-jawed chuck, and, for support, bring up the tailstock.

5

Reduce the square stock with a roughing gouge followed by a skew or the Spindlemaster.

6

Make sure the jam chuck is 1¼" in diameter or the block you drilled will not fit properly.

19

Place a ⅛" drill bit into a Jacobs Chuck and place the Jacobs Chuck into the tailstock.

20

Use the Jacobs Chuck as a drill to place a ⅛" hole in the bottom of the base to accommodate a finial.

21

Make a small finial for the bottom of the base, staining and finishing it in a manner similar to Step 18. Make sure that the tenon you create is ⅛" to fit into the base, and part it off with a parting tool.

22

Reduce another piece of wood for the roof to approximately 2" in diameter, and use a small spindle gouge to start to shape the roof of the birdhouse. Using a parting tool, make a small tenon on the underside of the roof to fit the body of the ornament.

23

Hollow out the inside of the roof using a small bowl gouge, making light cuts to remove wood from the inside to make the ornament lighter in weight. **Caution:** Do not remove too much material or you will go through the roof of the ornament.

24

Continue to remove wood, shaping the roof using a spindle gouge. For additional support, the tailstock is brought up to meet the roof section and some scrap Styrofoam is used. Make a small finial of your choice for the top of the roof, and carefully sand the piece. Delicately part the roof section off using your parting tool.

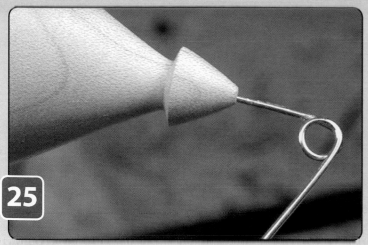

25 Place the roof piece into a jam chuck, and then use a safety pin or a very small numbered drill bit (#75) to make a hole in the top of the roof for the eye pin.

26 Use the blood-red stain to stain the roof, and then use the EEE Cream to remove the excess stain.

27 Apply woodturner's finish to the roof with a paper towel.

28 Glue the eye pin into the roof using CA glue, and allow it to dry thoroughly.

29 To make the perch, glue a small piece of wood no more than ½" in diameter and 1" long to a piece of scrap wood using CA glue. Turn it down to a finished size of ⁵⁄₁₆" on the outside of the perch and an overall length of ¾". Sand, stain, and finish the perch to your satisfaction. The tenon should be ⅛" in diameter to fit the hole that was created in Step 11.

30 Using a black marker or black acrylic paint, darken the inside of the ornament to give the illusion that it is big inside. Glue the perch in the perch hole, the base finial into the base, and the roof onto the main body of the ornament. If you choose, you can purchase small ornamental birds (any craft supply store has these) and glue one onto the perch.

Simple Lidded Box

Tools and Supplies

- Roughing gouge
- Skew or Spindlemaster
- Parting tool
- Round/side cutting scraper
- ³⁄₈" bowl gouge
- Four-jawed chuck
- Digital calipers
- Hollow form calipers
- 1½" Forstner drill bit with Jacobs Chuck
- Wood of choice (Bethlehem olive wood 3" x 3" x 6")
- Sanding pads and sandpaper in assorted grits
- EEE Cream and woodturner's finish
- Lathe (speed set to 500 to 2000 rpm)

People like boxes—big ones, small ones, any size and shape ones! At craft fairs or shows there can be a dozen intricately turned pieces, but one of the first items to be touched are the boxes. Curiosity gets the best of the customers, and they have to open the box to examine what is inside. As they open a box, they should hear that "pop" sound which assures a good, tight fit between the top and the body of the box.

When creating boxes of any shape and size, a general rule is to make the bottom of the box to the top of the box in a ratio of 3:5 or 3:4. In other words, if the overall height of the box is 5", the top should be approximately 1½" to 2", and the body of the box should be 3" to 3½". For your first box, the shape will be simple with a gradual, sloping cove in the top and the body of the box. When you are using a scraper for the inside of the box, remember to go slowly, taking small bites at a time.

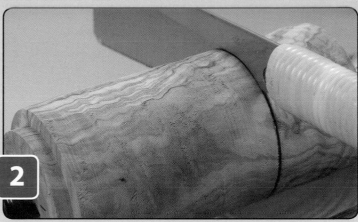

Start with a block of wood at least 3" x 3" x 5½" and reduce it to a cylinder approximately 3¼" in diameter using a roughing gouge. Draw a line 1½" from one end to establish the top of the box.

With a ¼" parting tool, make a large enough spigot on each end of the cylinder so a four-jawed chuck can hold the piece. Next, using a thin parting tool (¹⁄₁₆"), cut on the marked line, leaving approximately ½" to be cut with a small hand saw. Do not attempt to cut all the way through the cylinder with the parting tool! The parting tool will bind in the kerf and may cause damage to either the wood or yourself.

Lidded Box Tip:

To ensure a snug fit between the top and the body of the box, use pre-dried wood and measure often. In addition, you can use the body of the box to physically fit it to the top and vice versa to get that tight-fitting feel for the box. If you use "wet" wood, it will shrink, and the fit will be loose and possibly out of round when it dries.

Place the body of the box into the four-jawed chuck and bring up the tailstock for support. Turn a shallow cove in the body of the box.

Use a ¼" parting tool and create a flange for the top to rest on. Remove approximately ¼" of material, as illustrated.

Insert the 1¼" Forstner drill bit into the Jacobs Chuck and drill into the body of the box approximately 3¼".

6 Cutting from the hole that was just drilled, use a side cutting scraper to remove wood from the center of the box to the outer edges of the box, leaving ⅛" as a rim for the top of the box. Remember, the scraper should be just above the centerline of the piece. Scrape all the way to the bottom of the body of the box. The walls should be a uniform thickness and can be checked using the hollow form calipers.

7 Carefully sand the inside of the body of the box, being careful when your fingers are sanding inside the box.

8 Insert the top of the box into the four-jawed chuck and drill the center with the Forstner bit to a depth of 1¼" as you did with the body of the box.

9 With digital calipers, measure the outside flange on the body of the box.

10 Hollow out the top of the box as you did with the body of the box, noting that the inside diameter should just be a snug fit over the body of the box.

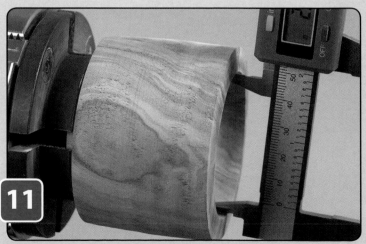

11 Stop frequently to measure the inside diameter to ensure a snug fit. If the scraping was correctly accomplished, a very light sanding is all that will be necessary. **Caution:** Do not over sand inside the top. The fit will not be snug.

12 Fit the two pieces together and use a cone-shaped revolving center in the tailstock to snug the pieces together to give a final shape to the box.

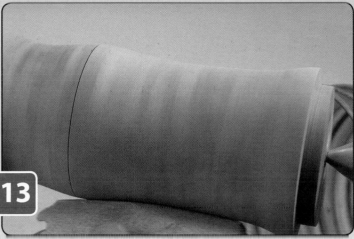

13 Sand the exterior of the box with sandpaper to 800 grit and then use sanding pads, such as Abralon pads. At this point, you can apply the EEE Cream and the woodturner's finish to the outside of the box as you have done in previous sections.

14 Reverse chuck the top into the four-jawed chuck, and, using a skew or Spindlemaster, turn the top spigot into a small finial. Sand and finish.

15 Reverse chuck the body of the box into the four-jawed chuck, and, using small bites and a ⅜" bowl gouge, remove the spigot on the bottom of the body of the box.

16 Slightly concave the bottom of the box and add a decoration of beads, coves, or lines. Apply the same finish to the bottom of the box as you did to the sides. Don't forget to sign your work.

17 The finished box.

Faceplate Turning
Natural Edge Bowl

Tools and Supplies

- ½" bowl gouge with fingernail profile
- Four-jawed chuck and worm screw
- Curved scraper
- Round nose scraper
- Double-ended calipers
- Wood of choice (6" in diameter x 4" thick)
- Sanding pads and sandpaper in assorted grits
- Turner's two-way tape (Do not use double-sided carpet tape—it will not be strong enough to hold at a high rate of spinning.)
- Tung oil (diluted with mineral spirits 4:1)
- Lathe (speed set to 500 to 2000 rpm)
- Two pieces of 2" foam insulation
- Piece of router mat or other thin, rubber-type material

Before we start, a word of caution is necessary when turning natural edge bowls.

- The edges are not even and therefore represent a hazard with the edges spinning at a fast rate. Always be aware of where your hands are in relation to the edges of the bowl blank. It only takes once, and, trust me, you will not forget about it again!

Four-jawed chuck and worm screw

- Remove any loose bark before it removes itself. There is nothing worse than getting hit in the chest with a big chunk of flying bark.

1

Because you used a template to cut out the bowl blank initially (see the Transforming Logs section on pages 18 and 19), you have a screw mark to use for the center on the bark side of your blank. Turn the blank over, place your template on the bottom of the blank, and use it as a guide for locating the center. Use an awl to make a center point.

2

Once the center points are located, place the blank in between the drive spur and the tailstock. Note the position of the tool rest because this will be useful in locating the high spots of the bowl blank.

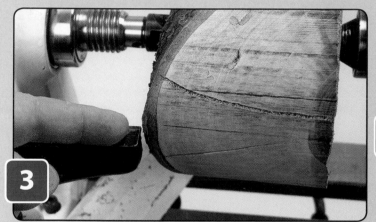

3

Turn the blank by hand until one edge of the blank comes close to the edge of the tool rest, as indicated by my finger. Keep a mental note where this piece of the bowl is in relation to the tool rest.

4

Rotate the blank 180 degrees to the opposite side of the blank and see how close this edge of the blank comes to the tool rest. Both sides should be equal distance from the tool rest. If one side is not, adjust the blank by moving the back end of the blank in the tailstock until they are equal. Now spin the blank by hand to make sure both sides are equal distance from the tool rest. Once they are equal, lock the tailstock down and tighten it into the blank to secure it firmly.

5

Adjust the height of the tool rest and turn the hand brake to ensure that your bowl blank will not hit the tool rest. Set your lathe to the slowest speed, around 500 rpm, and turn the lathe on. It will vibrate and shake (this is normal) because the blank is not round yet. Take a little off the sides using the bowl gouge to round the blank, and then square off the bottom to prepare it for the four-jawed chuck.

6

Continue to shape the blank, taking small bites and keeping in mind that the edge of the bowl is near your hand!

7

Use the bevel-cutting technique (ABC's) to remove small bites of wood from the blank and get a very smooth cut at the same time. Note the nice shavings coming off the gouge because the bevel is being supported by the bowl blank.

Natural Edge Bowl Tip:

Your best bet to keep the bark on a natural edge bowl is to acquire the tree pieces after the tree has stopped growing in the fall or in the winter before it starts to grow again. The bark is less likely to stay on the bowl when it is being turned if the tree was cut in the spring or summer when the tree is actively growing.

8

Form a spigot on the bottom of the bowl so the four-jawed chuck can securely grip the blank.

9

Place the blank into the four-jawed chuck and tighten the jaws around the spigot.

10

If there are visible cracks in the outside of the bowl blank, use thin CA glue and drip it into the cracks.

11

Even if the tree was cut in the fall, place some thin CA glue all around the edge of the bowl to assist in keeping the bark on the bowl blank when turning. Better safe than sorry!

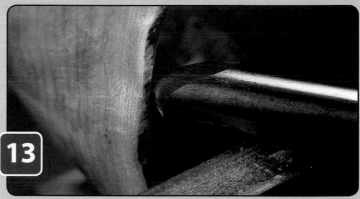

Make a final finishing cut on the outside of the bowl, and then use a power sander or an angle sander and sand the outside of the bowl at this time. Depending on how well you just made a final pass with the bowl gouge, start sanding with 100-grit paper, and then use the sanding pads as the final sanding step.

Place the gouge firmly on the tool rest. You will be cutting air when you first start to cut near the rim of the bowl. Make sure that the bevel of the gouge is parallel to the inside of the bowl each time you start your cut, and continue to push the gouge into the bowl, ensuring that the bevel of the gouge is supported by the bowl. The finished bowl was used for this picture to demonstrate how close you can get to the edge of the bowl and still have support for the bevel from the inside of the bowl.

The wall thickness should be established at this point. Continue taking small bites and work down the side of the bowl and then to the middle. Remove approximately 1" at a time so the fibers of the wood are supported by the ones below it.

When you get to the middle of the bowl, the bevel of the gouge should still be rubbing against the bottom of the bowl.

Check for equal wall thickness using the double-ended calipers frequently as you reduce the inside of the bowl. Remember to work down 1" at a time; that way the edge of the bowl is always supported.

There might be a little nub left on the inside of the bowl, as illustrated.

18

Remove the nub left at the bottom of the bowl using a round nose scraper. When using a scraper, you must be slightly above the centerline of the bowl. Remove the little nub and make sure that there is not a bump in the bottom of the bowl.

19

Use a curved scraper to lightly scrape the inside walls of the bowl to remove any tool marks that might be visible.

20

Sand the inside of the bowl using the wavy sanding disks, such as those from New Wave, to smooth out the interior of the bowl and to remove any tool marks. Sand your bowl to at least 800 grit to give it the best possible surface for finishing. **Tip:** Always use an angle sander or a power sanding attachment when sanding natural edge bowls. The spinning edges may tear your hands up if you try to sand by hand!

21

You can apply a finish to both the inside and the outside of the bowl at this point by leaving it in the chuck and rubbing tung oil on it with a soft, lint-free rag. Allow the tung oil to thoroughly dry before proceeding to the next step.

22

Before turning the bottom of the bowl, you will need to prepare a jam chuck for the inside of the bowl. Glue two pieces of 2" foam insulation together and use turner's two-way tape to mount this on your faceplate.

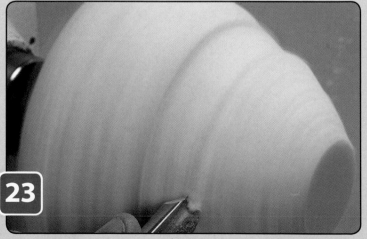

23

Turn the insulation to the general shape of the inside of the bowl and "ta-da"—you have a jam chuck made from insulation material.

24 Place a piece of router mat or some other type of thin, rubber-type material over the insulation; then, place the bowl over the rubber mat and bring up the tailstock for support.

25 A light touch is needed to remove the spigot on the bottom until you are left with a little piece still holding the bowl. Add a little decoration to the bottom of the bowl such as lines or small coves.

26 Sand the bottom of the bowl, being careful not to apply too much pressure and dislodge the bowl from the jam chuck.

27 Leave the bowl in the jam chuck you made and use a small gouge to remove the nub left on the bottom and sand it to your satisfaction.

28 Coat the bowl with diluted tung oil and allow it to thoroughly dry before buffing with a buffing system.

29 The finished natural edge bowl.

Faceplate Turning
End-grain Hollow Vessel

Tools and Supplies

- Roughing gouge
- ½" bowl gouge
- Skew or Spindlemaster
- Parting tool
- Round nose scraper
- Hollowing tool and hollow form calipers
- Four-jawed chuck
- Jacobs Chuck with 1" drill bit
- Wood of choice (orange agate, 4" x 4" x 9" long)
- Sanding pads and sandpaper in assorted grits
- Lathe (speed set to 500 to 2000 rpm)
- Diluted tung oil (diluted with mineral spirits 4:1)

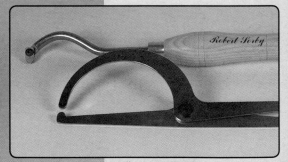

Hollowing tool and hollow form calipers

When hollowing out an end-grain vessel, an initial hole is bored into the center of the vessel to an established depth, and then wood is removed from the center of the vessel toward the outside edge by using scrapers. This is opposite from bowl turning where you are working from the outside edge, removing wood toward the center by riding the bevel of a bowl gouge.

For your first vessel, a simple but elegant shape has been chosen. It will have a large opening at the top of the vessel to accommodate a variety of tools and to ensure a successful outcome. Trying to work through a very small opening for your first vessel may become a daunting task, and the objective here, for your first vessel, should be the mechanics of turning rather than turning the most impressive, lightest, and most intricately shaped vessel.

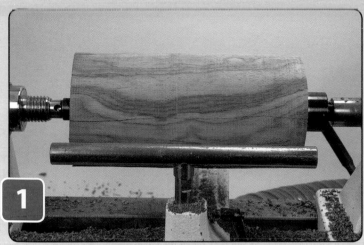

Reduce the square stock to a round cylinder using a roughing gouge and then a skew.

Using a parting tool, make a spigot on each end of the round stock to accommodate the opening of your four-jawed chuck.

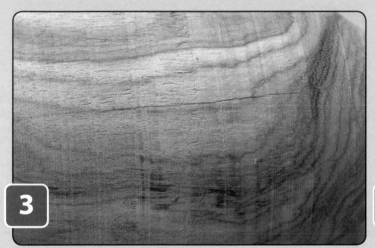

While reducing the square stock, you might encounter cracks in the wood. Don't panic; keep removing wood until the cracks disappear. If you do end up removing wood because of cracks, your vessel will simply be a little narrower than you originally planned.

Sand the outside of the vessel using the power sanding method.

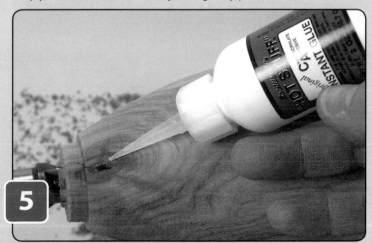

If you encounter minor inclusions and cracks in the wood that would take too much shape from your vessel, fill them with some CA glue and sawdust mix to prevent the cracks from spreading or the holes from becoming larger.

Reverse the vessel and place it into the four-jawed chuck. Bring up the tailstock to make sure that the vessel is running true. If necessary, adjust the vessel in the four-jawed chuck to ensure that the piece is well balanced.

7

Once the vessel is secured by the four-jawed chuck, use a parting tool to remove the spigot that was left on the top of the piece.

8

Place a ½" drill bit into a Jacobs Chuck and drill the center of the vessel. I drilled in about 5". To ensure that the walls do not crack, they should be the same thickness as the bottom.

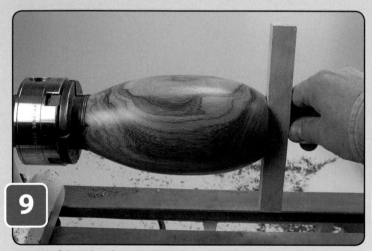

9

A piece of dowel and a straight stick can be used as a depth gauge to check the penetration of the drill bit.

10

Remove the dowel and the stick and place them on top of the vessel to see how deep the drill bit penetrated the vessel. Remember, the thickness of the bottom of the vessel should be approximately the same as the wall thickness.

11

With a round nose scraper, start hollowing out the piece from the center of the hole you made with the drill bit to the outside edge of the vessel. Take very light bites to avoid catches and digs.

12

As you go deeper inside the vessel, it will be harder to control the scraper. Move the tool rest inside the vessel to assist in keeping the scraper just above the centerline of the piece. To assist in seeing inside the vessel, an additional light source may be required.

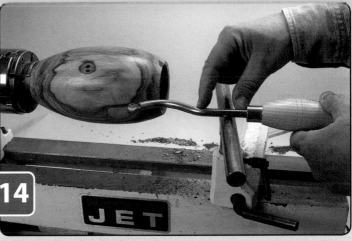

The wall thickness should be established at this time when first starting to scrape the inside of the piece. Consistent wall thickness will reduce the likelihood that the vessel will crack.

Depending on the size of the opening you have established, you may need to use a special hollowing tool. The proper way to use this tool is to ensure that the straight portion of the tool is always supported by the tool rest, as indicated by my fingers.

The hollowing tool is taking small bites, working from the inside of the hole to the outside edge, ensuring that the curved part of the tool does not come into contact with the tool rest. If that happens, the tool will roll over and a catch will occur.

Continue removing wood from the inside of the vessel, working from the inside hole that was made to the outside edge of the vessel, frequently checking for consistent wall thickness.

After the wall thickness and depth are uniform, remove the vessel and reverse chuck it into the four-jawed chuck.

Use a small bowl gouge and a very light touch to remove the spigot that was left on the bottom of the vessel and to slightly concave the bottom.

19

Apply any decorative beads, coves, or lines you want to add to the bottom of the vessel.

20

An instructor of mine always painted the inside of his vessels with black acrylic paint to create an illusion of depth. In reality, it also served his purpose to hide the imperfections that might be visible.

21

Here is the finished end-grain hollow vessel created from orange agate wood.

Marketing and Selling Your Work

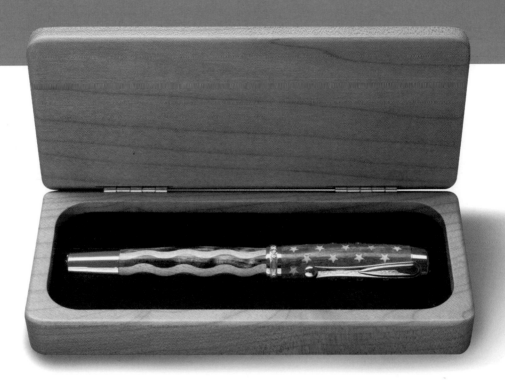

How many pieces of your work can you have in the house? After the bedroom, living room, bathroom, guest room, and even the kid's room all have an original, one-of-a-kind turned piece and all of your friends and family have your work, it's time to look at the possibility of selling some of your treasures.

So where do you begin? In the next few pages, some of the answers will start to take shape, and hopefully a few solid ideas will get you motivated to free your home of all of those pieces that have been collecting.

There are volumes of books written on marketing your work. This is by no means a slam-dunk, surefire few pages of pure golden knowledge on the subject. It is a realistic approach on how to offer your work for sale, where to sell it, the best way to display it, and a way to value it for sale.

Marketing

So let's start with the dirty little "M" word. Marketing—there, I said it! A dirty word to most, but to me it means "Money."

Marketing is evolving all of the time, constantly changing. One day marketing may be advertising, the next day it may be selling, and the next day it may mean trying to contact other people concerning your work. Marketing is anything to do with your business and the business of promoting your product. You are marketing all the time without realizing it. Each time you speak with someone concerning your turnings, you are effectively marketing your work. Do not be ashamed to tell people what you do in your spare time. I have been a sales manager in the medical industry for over 25 years, and I cannot tell you how many times I have sold items to physicians simply because I mentioned to them what I did in my spare time.

The more people know you and your work, the better off you will be. The best sales to me are the word-of-mouth sales and the repeat sales from prior customers.

Points of sale

The first question you must answer is, "Where can I sell my work?" The answer is simple: Ask other turners either where they display their work or what shows they attend.

Attend craft shows and other local artisan shows to see what is being offered in your area. When you attend these shows, see what the turners are selling and what prices they are charging. Ask the turners if they are selling any of their products. Examine how they have their turnings

When setting up for a show, do not be shy about promoting yourself. A banner with your name on it demonstrates to the public who you are. Also, lighting your work is a must. Bright lights will show how well your products are finished. Ever notice that a diamond looks better in a jewelry store than at home? The difference is the lighting!

displayed. Take in the whole experience of the show; watch the people—are they buying or just kicking tires? If they are buying, what are they buying and how much are they spending? By the way, as you are observing these things, guess what—you are marketing! So the "M" word is starting to look better.

Let's take a moment to examine craft shows. There are many types of craft shows and fairs. You will hear of juried shows and non-juried shows. A juried show is one where you have to present either your actual work or good-quality 35mm slides representative of your work to a group of people who will judge if the quality of your work is good enough to be in their show. Usually a juried show will bring higher prices for your work because a more affluent crowd of people will attend, knowing the quality of workmanship will be good.

Listen to your customers...

You were born with two ears and one mouth, so listen twice as much as you speak! Ask questions and take a moment to listen to what your customers want. If you find that the market in your area loves natural edge bowls, then you will have a difficult time selling them open-ended vessels. As customers walk by your booth, greet them, invite them in, and then listen to what they have to say. Once they are in your booth, are your items well lighted? There is nothing more frustrating than having a beautiful quilted bowl that is so poorly lighted that the customers cannot see the shine of your finish! Speaking of sales, make sure that your customer knows you take credit cards. Many sales have been made due to the fact that credit cards were accepted.

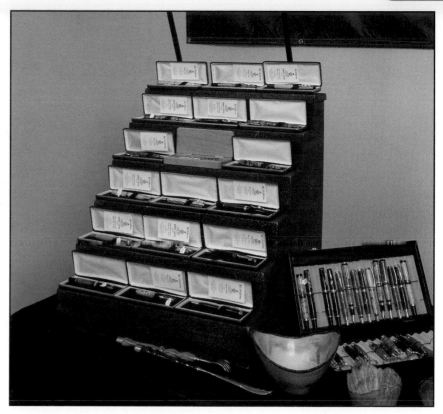

Keep your display clean, neat, and well organized.

Wholesale versus retail?

Do you want to go to craft fairs or just put your work in a few shops and let someone else sell your work? One key thing to remember is that no one can sell your work like you can! When I first started out, I placed my work all over in upscale boutiques and shops on consignment. I can tell you that this was a disaster! I lost more items because these shops would sell the items and not pay me or go out of business and take my merchandise. Many bad things can happen when your work is on consignment, so my tendency is to sell retail at upscale craft fairs.

As an experiment, I placed my work with a friend, and he went to a large show in Washington, D.C. He had items similar to mine, and he sold 18 items of his and only one of mine. At the next large show, in Philadelphia, I took his work with me. This time I sold 16 pieces of my work and none of his! If you are selling to the

When you are at shows or fairs, let the public touch your product. Let them "feel" the quality of your work. While they are holding a piece, tell them how it is made, what type of wood you used, and any other relevant information you feel will help to sell your product.

public, they like to buy directly from the artisan themselves. No one can sell your work like yourself. I tell humorous (at least I think they are) stories of how the turning was made and what type of wood it is, where it comes from, and a lot of other details that only I can know. It is the personal touch of that "M" word, and people like it!

Pricing: the touchy part of the "M" thing

What do I charge for this widget? While you are at the various craft fairs, you are studying prices to see what the market will tolerate. What the market will tolerate and what you want to charge may be two entirely different things.

One item artists tend to overlook is their time. Time is money! Your time has a value, and you should not diminish the fact that you did spend the time making the piece. If people want cheap,

they're probably not going to appreciate a hand turned piece, so let them buy a knock-off bowl. You are creating one-of-a-kind, handmade items and should be compensated accordingly.

A simple formula for pricing is: PRICE = cost of material + overhead + labor + profit. What was the cost of the material? A friend told you to come over and help take the tree down, so the wood was free, right? How about the time you spent cutting the tree down and the time and gas you consumed going to his house? All of these factors have to come into play when figuring actual cost of material.

The overhead is the cost of your tools, heat, electricity, insurance, and rent. If you are using one room in your home to produce these items, then you may want to obtain a total cost of the room over the period of a year and then divide this by the number of pieces you actually turned.

Labor is time, and time is money. What is the local shop rate for a handyman in your area: $20, $45, $75 per hour? You have to place a value on your time, but you also have to be realistic. You are not a brain surgeon, so do not charge like one!

Profit—the "P" word. You are allowed to make money, and the person who is buying your product knows that; however, since you have charged a fair price, they are willing to pay for your item. A fair percentage profit is 30 percent. Let's say that, after figuring all of the above factors, a bowl cost you $45 to produce. Add 30 percent of $45, or $13-$14, and the total cost to the consumer is $59.

Once you have established what prices you will charge for your work, you can determine where to be in the food chain of craft shows or upscale boutiques. By following some of these guidelines for marketing, you can take the "M" word and make some money.

Gallery

As beginners, we look to the more experienced turners and ask how did they do that or, more importantly, where did they get the idea to create that particular piece? As you become more experienced with turning, you will understand, as you are creating a bowl or vessel, that you can ask yourself, "What if I did it this way?" or "What if I change this a little over here?" By experimenting and changing the methods you use, you will grow as a turner. If you like what you just accomplished, write it down so you will not forget how you did it. In time, you will see that your technique and style will undergo a metamorphosis, and you will see more clearly how experienced turners do what they do! The following pages will demonstrate some unique ideas in turning.

Dave Hardy

Dave has been teaching and demonstrating nationally since 1977. He has won numerous awards, and some of his most popular and better-known turnings are his castles. The base of this castle is made from mahogany. The ground that the castle sits on is big leaf maple burl that has been washed with green acrylic paint. The walls of the castle are cherry wood. A woodburning tip is used to create the illusion of windows and doors. The castle roofs are all made from walnut.

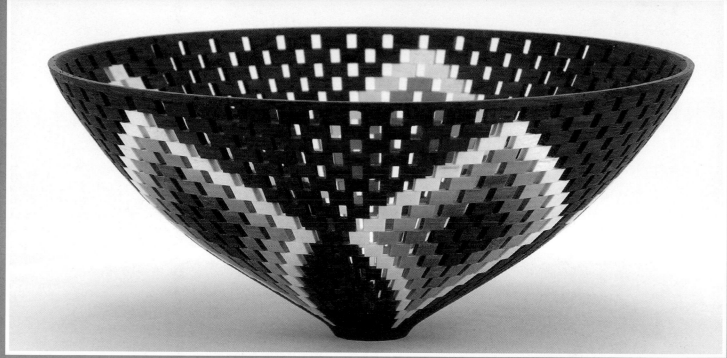

This piece is 3" high by 5" in width and is constructed from padauk, holly, pear, and chakpe viga.

William Smith

Segmented turning has been around a long time; however, one of the newest aspects of turning is open segmented turning. Bill Smith has recently published a book on open segmented turning and has graciously shared some of his works for this publication.

This first piece, which is 3" tall and 4½" wide, is made from purpleheart and holly. To really appreciate the beauty of this piece, as well as all of Bill's work, the bowl should be viewed from the top down.

Constructed from bloodwood, ebony, and holly, this piece is 5½" high by 3½" wide.

Derek Wildman

Barely out of his teens and wining praise and admiration from turners, Derek is an artist on the rise who has focused his attention to turning and carving.

Ghost is his latest creation, standing 8" high by 6" wide, made from Norfolk Island pine. This piece was first turned on a lathe and then carved to offer the details you see.

Michael Kagan
Michael is another example of an artist who turns a piece first and then carves his design.

This vessel, 5" tall by 3½" wide, uses catalpa for the body of the vessel with an ebony accent opening.

Michael also likes to work in miniatures, such as these acorn boxes made from cocobolo and boxwood on the left and one made from blackwood and sandalwood on the right.

Bill Sarver

Bill Sarver teaches turning and more recently has focused his attention on the surface treatments of his works. His vessels are delicately shaped and are then treated with acrylic paints.

This cherry vessel is 10" tall by 4½" wide, with black and white accents on the top of the vessel.

This piece is a maple vessel, 10" tall by 4½" wide, painted with acrylic white and black paint.

Barry Gross

A woodworker for more than 30 years, Barry turns primarily pens and small bowls. He often combines wood with other materials to create his unique pieces.

This natural edge ambrosia maple bowl is 6" high by 4½" wide.

This box has a Bethlehem olive wood bottom and a cocobolo lid. It is 4" high by 2½" wide.

This oil-filled kaleidoscope is made of cocobolo and is 9 ½" long by 1½" wide.

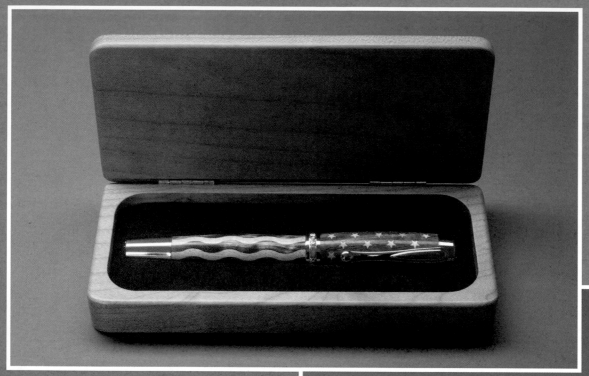

The *Stars & Stripes Pen* has 50 stars and 13 stripes exactly as a real American flag does. This pen was made for the Speaker of the House of Representatives, Senator Dennis Hastert.

This snakewood bowl with a bit of sapwood showing measures 1½" high by 3" wide.

This bowl was turned from eucalyptus burl and measures 1½" high by 3½" wide.

Troubleshooting

One of the first rules in turning that you must accept is, "Things happen!" You are turning a perfectly solid piece of wood, and suddenly a void appears; you lose your concentration for a second, and a catch happens. Now you have a choice: You can throw a temper tantrum, kick the wall, and break your toe (I can tell you that it hurts) or you can do a sudden "redesign" on the shape of the piece to cover up the indiscretion!

We all make mistakes; even the finest, most accomplished turners will make a mistake. The secret is to learn from the error and avoid making the same blunder again.

Problem 1: What if my piece breaks?

The striking, quilted maple bowl pictured on this page did not start out in this shape; it ended up this way (see **Photo 1A**). The thickness of the wall was not measured enough, and, as a result, a piece of the bowl was cut off (see **Photo 1B**)! Rather than scrap this beautiful piece of wood, the bowl was made smaller, and when it is sold, no one except me will ever know that this shape was not the original shape intended for this bowl (see **Photo 1C**)!

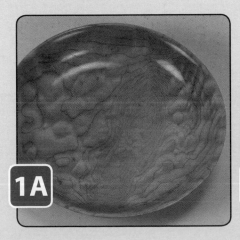

Problem 2: How do I fix catches and small breaks?

This Bethlehem olive wood box started out to be a straight box all the way down with no shape whatsoever. My cat found her way into the shop and knocked over something. I turned slightly, and, in the blink of an eye, my skew dug into the wood with a huge catch. After "gently" removing the cat from the shop, I shaped the box with coves to get rid of the catch. The results are shown in **Photo 2A.**

Unfortunately, this is not the only thing to happen to this box. I was at a show displaying the box when it was knocked to the ground. Since the edges on the top and bottom were sharp edges, a piece of the top edge broke off. Very nicely, I informed the person that I could fix it with no trouble and not to worry. The piece was remounted into a four-jawed chuck, and the top was reshaped as shown in **Photo 2B**. The original shape was better, but this is still a very saleable piece.

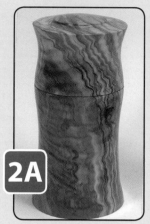

Problem 3: What do I do if sudden cracks appear?

The first question you need to ask yourself is, "Where are the cracks located?" Are they heat induced or are they cracks within the wood? If the cracks were heat induced because the walls of the piece are thin, sanding is probably the culprit, as illustrated with this ambrosia maple bowl (see **Photo 3A**). Thin CA glue was used to bond the piece together (see **Photo 3B**). The bowl was lightly sanded and the result is demonstrated in **Photo 3C**. Once the rest of the bowl is sanded and a finish is applied, the repair will not be noticeable.

If the cracks are deep within the wood, then placing thin CA glue into the crack will "assist" in keeping the piece together (see **Photo 3D**). The key word here is "assist" in keeping it together, not "definitely will" keep it together. Sometimes the wood is too far gone to save. In this particular instance, it did work.

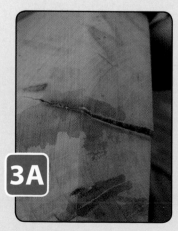

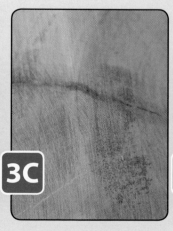

Problem 4: How can I repair large cracks?

Currently on the market there are many commercial inlay materials from which to choose. Some of the choices are Inlace metal dust, turquoise rounds and nuggets, and many crushed stone powders, such as peridot, iron pyrite, malachite, galena, and azurite. Filling cracks with crushed stone or other inlay products is an excellent technique to cover the void (see **Photo 4A**). Use a rotary tool to enlarge the crack to accept the crushed turquoise stone (see **Photo 4B**). Fill the enlarged crack with thin CA glue as a base to seal the crack (see **Photo 4C**). Next, place the pieces of crushed stone into the crack (see **Photo 4D**). Place medium CA glue on top of the crushed stone and allow it to dry. Do not use any accelerator on the CA glue because the accelerator will cause air bubbles; allow the CA glue to dry on its own. Fill in any voids with more medium CA glue if necessary (see **Photo 4E**). Sand the piece as you normally would and apply the finish of your choice (see **Photo 4F**).

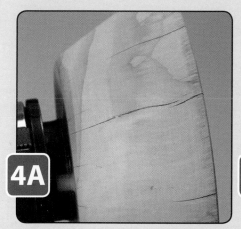

4A

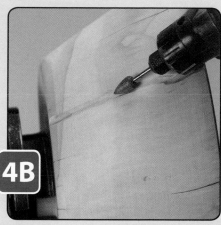

4B

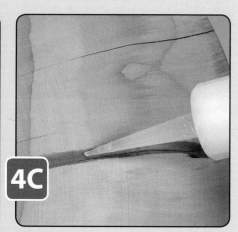

4C

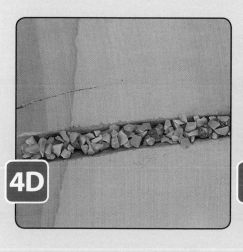

4D

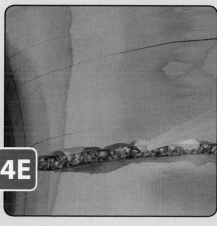

4E

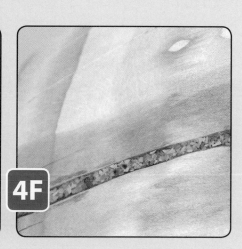

4F

Problem 5: Why are there cracks in my bowl?

The bowl blank was prepared wrong; the blank was cut from the end of the log with the pith in the center, and the wall thickness was not uniform with the bottom of the bowl.

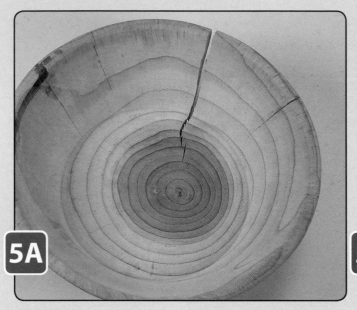

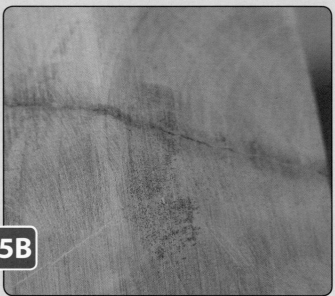

Problem 6: What if I chipped off a piece of my pen blank?

The first objective is to retrieve the missing piece. Once that is found, use a medium viscosity CA glue to glue the chipped-off piece back into the pen blank (see **Photos 6A** and **6B**).

Pen blanks made from burls can have a lot of voids in them, depending on the particular wood burl that is being used. If this occurs, use some of the wood shavings from that particular pen blank and mix them with CA glue to glue into the void (see **Photo 6C**).

Problem 7: What if the jam chuck I prepared is too loose?

Do not discard it. Just place a piece of paper towel on top of the jam chuck, and then put your workpiece on top of that.

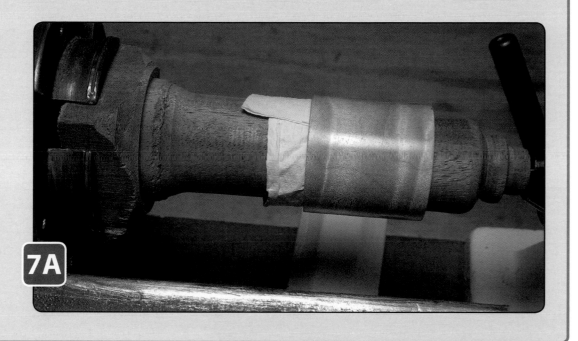

7A

Problem 8: How to I unclog the tips on the CA glue ?

Place the tip in a container of acetone, and, when you need a fresh tip, there is always one available.

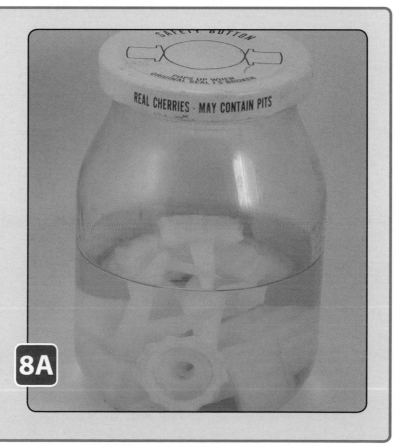

8A

Company Resources listed alphabetically:

Arizona Silhouette
1224 South 37th Drive
Yuma, AZ 85364
(928) 329–8039

Behlen's Stains & Finishes
RPM Wood Finishes Group
PO Box 3190
Hickory, NC 28603
1–800–545–0047

Berea Hardwoods Co., Inc.
18745 Sheldon Road
Middleburg Heights, OH 44130
1–877–736–5487

BG Artforms
2189 Philip Drive
Bensalem, PA 19020
1–888–717–4202

Craft Supply USA
1287 East 1120 South
Provo, UT 84606
1–800–551–8876

Ironclad Performance Wear
12506 Beatrice Street
Los Angeles, CA 90066
1–888–314–3197

New Edge Cutting Tools
PO Box 282
Plantsville, CT 06479
(860) 628–4642

Packard Woodworks
PO Box 718
Tryon, NC 28782
1–800–683–8876

Penn State Industries
9900 Global Road
Philadelphia, PA 19115
1–800–377–7297

Rings & Things
1–800–366–2156

Trend Airshield Respirator & Air Ace
Trend USA
Suite R
1220 Corporation Parkway
Raleigh, NC 27610
(859) 485–2080

Triton Powered Respirator
Triton Woodworking Systems
PO Box 523
Cornwall, ON K6H-5T2
Canada
1–888–874–8661

Wagner Electronic Products
(Moisture Meter)
326 Pine Grove Road
Rogue River, OR 97537
1–800–634–9961

Woodcraft Corporation
1177 Rosemar Road
Parkersburg, WV 26102
(304) 422–5412

Glossary of Helpful Terms

Banjo: Secures the tool rest to the lathe bed.

CA Glue, or Cyanoacrylate Glue: Also called Super Glue. An adhesive that is available in various viscosities (thin, medium, and gap filling).

Calipers: Used to set diameters on spindle work.

Carbide Cutting Tools: Tools that utilize carbide integrated into the tools.

Chuck: A device used to hold a piece of wood firmly to the end of the spindle in the headstock end of the lathe when faceplate operations are carried out such as bowl turning.

Collet Chuck: A type of chuck jaw that is closed by the action of a tapered chuck ring.

Drill Chuck, or Jacobs Chuck: A three-jawed drill chuck used to hold twist drills and other bits made for drilling holes. Fits into the Morse taper socket in the headstock or tailstock.

Drive Spur: Supports the wood at the spindle end and has four prongs and a point that drives the workpiece around.

Faceplate Turning: Used to describe the turning of bowls or plates where the grain is usually at right angles to the axis of the lathe and where there is no tailstock support.

Faceplate: A metal disc that threads onto the spindle and has screw holes for attaching the wood to the faceplate for turning.

Green Wood Turning: Turning freshly cut wood that will have a high moisture content.

Headstock: The part of the lathe that is driven by the motor and where a chuck or a faceplate can be mounted.

Indexing: Used to divide a circle of rotation into equal divisions.

Kiln-Dry Lumber: Lumber that has been dried commercially to speed up the natural drying process.

Lathe Bed: The lower portion of the lathe that keeps all of the components of the lathe rigidly aligned.

Live Center, or Tailstock Center vs. a Dead Center: Located in the tailstock, a live center contains bearings that support the end of the wood and allows it to rotate. A dead center has a fixed point and does not rotate.

Mandrel, Pen Mandrel: A precision-machined steel bar that is held into the headstock of the lathe to hold the bushings and pen blanks needed to make a pen.

Morse Taper: A tapered hole located in both the spindle end and in the tailstock barrel. Morse tapers are either a #1 or a #2.

N.G.R. Stain: A non-grain-raising type of dye stain that contains no binders or solids and is usually soluble in alcohol. It usually refers to a dye stain that does not raise the grain of the wood.

Pin Chuck: A kind of chuck that grips into a predrilled hole.

Pith: Small, spongy part in the center of a log.

Quill: Inside the tailstock is a sliding barrel or "quill" that can be moved in or out by turning the handwheel.

Reverse Chucking: Turning the workpiece around and regripping it to gain access to the reverse side.

Screw Chuck: A faceplate with a single central screw used for quick mounting of simple projects where a central screw hole is acceptable.

Swing-Over Lathe Bed: Refers to the height of the largest object that may be turned without the object hitting the lathe bed.

Swivel Head: A headstock that can pivot around its vertical axis, allowing larger-diameter turning.

Tailstock: A housing that supports the end of the workpiece and can be moved along the lathe bed to suit different lengths of workpieces.

Tool Rest: Where the turning tool is placed before it comes into contact with the wood that is being turned. The height of the tool rest should be close to the height of your elbow as it relaxes by your side.

Worm Screw: Used to screw into a turning blank and then that is inserted into a four-jawed chuck.

Index

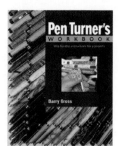
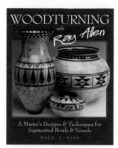
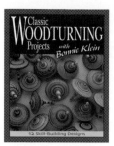
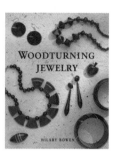
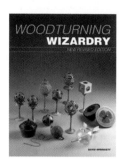
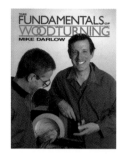
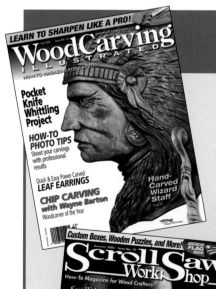